D0394341

Also by Jill Kargman

Sprinkle Glitter on My Grave

observations, rants, and other
uplifting thoughts about life

ballantine books
new york

Sprinkle Glitter on My Grave

written and *doodled* by

Jill Kargman

Published in the United States by Ballantine Books,
an imprint of Random House, a division of
Penguin Random House LLC, New York.

BALLANTINE and the HOUSE colophon are registered
trademarks of Penguin Random House LLC.

Grateful acknowledgment is made to
Rabbi Jack Riemer and Rabbi Sylvan Kamens
for permission to reprint the poem "We Remember Them"
(poem based on a nineteenth-century English poem).
Reprinted by permission of the authors.

ISBN 978-0-399-59457-1
ebook ISBN 978-0-399-59458-8

Printed in the United States of America on acid-free paper

randomhousebooks.com

9 8 7 6 5 4 3

Book design by Elizabeth A. D. Eno

Dead-icated to my family—I'm so lucky to spend life
(and eternity) by your sides. I love you so, xo jk

Contents

Sprinkle Glitter on My Grave

SPRINKLE GLITTER ON MY GRAVE 💀

We might appear to be normal human beings, but in truth, my family is the Munsters. We used to be the Addams Family, but when my brother married a sunny Southern California bride, I now think of us as the knockoff comedic goth family, because they had that one normal blonde, too. I'm not quite sure if she was the WASPy cousin or some wholesome niece, but she didn't seem to notice the Munsters' creepiness at all; that is, until her suitors ran screaming from her doorstep when her frankenservant cracked the lead-studded haunted house portal.

Okay, we don't have a doorbell that plays death knells, or a severed limb as a butler; we don't have a butler. But we are pretty morbid and Reaper obsessed. As children, when my brother, Willie, and I argued—typical sibling disagreements—my dad would stop our nonsense short with morbidness: *"Hey! When Mom and I kick the bucket, you're gonna be all each other's got, so knock it off!"*

We were in preschool, BTdubs.

The result? Sobs. Hysterical snot-bubble bawling in our feetie pajamas. And yet he always said that every time we'd bicker.

When he went on European business trips, he usually took the Concorde—his company sprang for it when he had to go to meetings that required him to arrive looking alive. But he never liked that supersonic plane. "One of these days," he'd say every time, "that pig's gonna blow and I just hope I'm not on it when it does." Tragically and memorably, he was right, that pig did blow (though without him on it).

We skied every Christmas and would be warned to be careful, because every year "Someone takes a header and rams into a tree and that's it."

He talked disease. Drunk driving. Choking mid-steak. We had conversations about The End all the time. He liked to discuss who was dying or who just looked like they had one foot in the grave. ("I ran into Bob today. He looks like he's on his way out.")

Sunday nights were our family eat-out night, usually Chinese. He'd often have just one more dumpling, because "Hey, we're all gonna be pushin' daisies someday." His attitude wasn't a cheesy you only live once–type bullshit that some people use to justify hedonistic behavior; it's not like he encouraged me to go get high on Venice Beach or told my brother to roll a condom on that dick before it's dust. His attitude was actually joyful. He was and is a firm believer in making the most of our time here, being productive, having strong human connections, and enjoying every day—not as our last per se, but because our days will one day run out.

His zest for life rubbed off. Rather than make us neurotics who were scared of life, all this talk and acknowledgment of death made my brother and me embrace every morsel of life. Morbidity doesn't have to be fear inducing—au contraire, it made us drink life to the lees (after we turned twenty-one, of course) and relish every bite of food. We cherished music. We flipped on the lights and immediately flipped on the radio. We sucked the marrow out of anything that appealed to the desperate-for-fuel senses and always tried to savor memories of all that is fleeting and ephemeral.

As adults, we still have this zest for life and the same dark humor. Willie has a tattoo up both his arms in a beautiful black script: *Mors certa, non vita*, Latin for "Death is certain, life is not." Now we both have kids of our own—nuggetini, we like to say—and we're both still trying to filch as much joy as we can out of our lives, and now, our children's fleeting childhoods. And maybe we're passing on the tradition.

My kids aren't afraid of spooky things because they've been exposed to them their whole little lives. I have art with skulls and hourglasses all around our house, and my kids don't blink.

But one time, a little pal of my daughter Sadie's was sleeping over and woke up in the middle of the night after a nightmare. With tears streaming down her face, she pitter-pattered into our room and burrowed into bed with me and my sleeping husband. "Mrs. Kargman, I'm scared of your house, there are so many *skeledins*," she said. I cuddled her and told her they don't have to be scary if you think of them as just part of us. I took her on a tour of the house and we greeted every skeleton, giving them each a silly name. Then I tucked her in with us, so she wouldn't be lonely beside my comatose daughters, and she fell asleep feeling better. Harry, my husband, was a little shocked when he woke up with a kid in our bed who was not our own. Actually that's putting it mildly. I think he said, *Um, what the fuck is this kid doing in our bed?* But when I explained it to him, he understood; he was once new to my family, too, and he found my Morticia side odd then, but now he totally gets it. My awesome little collection of hourglasses used to freak him out—they reminded him that time was constantly ebbing away—but now he understands the way I see that fragile shelf grouping: Time passing is constant, so don't sweat the small shit, don't wish away periods of time, enjoy it all. And we pretty much do.

Just as my parents have done for as long as I can remember, I reach first for the obituary section in *The New York Times*. And I'm not only interested in the cadavers who got headlines, I'm into the microscopic listy bodies, too. No matter the length or size of the font, I love stories of a life well lived and get inspired by what people made of their time on earth. Building on Billy Crystal's idea in *When Harry Met Sally . . .* to combine the obits with the real estate section: "He leaves two sons, seven grandchildren, and a sprawling prewar penthouse with wraparound terrace." Now that real estate has gone online, I think that's a very good editorial suggestion, too.

A few years ago, my parents bought cemetery plots for the family and announced with pride that we'd have a plum ocean view. Since then, they've logged many hours looking at tombstones on Pinterest. They scrutinized fonts and interviewed a few carvers before settling on the artisan who would create what will essentially be their business card for eternity. It was around that time that Harry and I realized it was time to begin in earnest a discussion about burial with our kids, Sadie, Ivy, and Fletch. After explaining to her what a burial plot is and what a headstone commemorates, Ivy, who was four at the time, said, "Mommy, when you die, I'm going to sprinkle glitter on your grave." I was shocked by this pronouncement. Had this kid been thinking of this for some time or had it just occurred to her? I asked her why this would be her plan. "Because," she replied, "you are sparkly and *fabulous* like glitter. Plus, glitter is very hard to clean up, so it will always be there."

Do I need to itemize the many reasons why I love this response? I don't think so. If you're a parent you get it—what an amazing sentiment and from such a happily morbid little person. Please consider this page part of my last will and testament. I can't think of a more badass or groovy plan for commemorating my crossing the river Styx than Ivy's amazing plan.

Incidentally, said plots are on Nantucket island, off the coast of Massachusetts. Neighboring island Martha's Vineyard happens to be the resting place for the genius comedian John Belushi. His tombstone is marked with hundreds of candy wrappers his fans continue to leave for him. I remember visiting as a child and thought it was cool and hilarious because I worshipped him, but actually, now that I think of it, it's cool but . . . kind of litter. And I prefer glitter.

DYING TO GET IN

Originally, we didn't get accepted into that perfectly manicured cemetery on Nantucket. When I heard we had been turned down, I imagined a board of trustees made entirely of skeletons sitting at a large dais with gavels in their bony paws, enthusiastically stamping REJECTED on our Kopelman family file, like the parole board in *Shawshank* who denied Morgan Freeman. Except they were all dead white peeps.

Turns out that the head of the cemetery (the head skeleton on the board) was named Mr. Morash. I swear on a stack of Zagat guides that this is true! If that's not the most hilarious *euonym* I don't know what is.

(*Note:* I am not a vocab snob. I didn't even know what the fuck *euonym* meant until it was the national spelling bee winning word in 1997. I had to look it up. It means a person whose name is what they do, like how my best friend Vanessa's ear doctor was named Dr. Listener. So, Mr. Morash? As in "more ash." More ashes. More dead people.)

I used this ego-bruising kerfuffle with Mr. Morash and his posse as the rough plot line for the third episode of *Odd Mom Out*, wherein I go berserk trying to score a coveted plot, lamenting the fact that I not only need to beat the odds to get my kid into a New York City kindergarten but also have to compete to be in the right worm buffet!

Back to real life: It is an understatement to say that it was insulting that our not-yet-but-one-day-to-be rigor mortised selves were somehow deemed unworthy of that Nantucket real estate. I was just a little tiny bit fucking outraged and my dad was clear that he and my mom, Coco, were *not* going to rot for eternity near JFK Airport. They decided to go on what was basically a college tour, but for cemeteries. But instead of four years, it was forever. Sadly, though, none held a candle to the one they wanted on Nantucket.

How'd we pull it off, then? No one likes a name-dropper, but drop a name I must: Former presidential candidate, U.S. senator, and secretary of state John Kerry—who is married to my godmother, Teresa Heinz—wrote a letter to the cemetery on our behalf. I don't know if they shuffled some bones or what, but his recommendation magically landed us some land to disintegrate in. According to Ginia Bellafante's *New York Times* article on the subject of hot, sold-out graveyards, people want to mingle with famous bodies buried nearby. It's like being a social climber in death. I guess some people just have networking in their bones.

The deeds were sent over, and while I was relieved everyone was relieved, I was still annoyed that connections matter, even in the Hereafter.

"That's life," my dad said, shrugging. And death, apparently.

My dad was euphoric when he saw our actual resting places.

"Guess what!" he marveled post-tour. "We got the best possible plots—right on the ocean! It has the best view in the entire place."

"But, Dad . . . we'll be dead."

"*Still!* Great location."

We laugh about this now, but what do you think John Kerry actually said in that letter of reference? Given his pedigree and his political representation of the state in which my carcass is now (thanks to him) destined to spend eternity, he could have just sent a text that said "Please take these people," and it might've worked.

But I think he might have had some fun with it. I know I would have. Here, for your reading pleasure, is my impersonation of the letter that John Kerry could have/should have mailed to gain us admission to that very special, members-only, WASP-island resting place:

Dear Mr. Morash,

I'm writing on behalf of my friends the Kopelman family, to recommend they rest in peace in your esteemed boneyard. I know they're New Yorkers, but I can assure you they will not be as loud after they pass on. Their children, William and Jill, will only leave the nicest of flower arrangements for their parents, and such will be the instructions to all Kopelman visitors to come—a tacky carnation shall never pass your gates. The Kopelmans understand they would be interred with descendants of the Mayflower *and would respectfully curb their Jewish gabbing to lend tranquillity to your beautiful stone garden. They will also curb their lifetime enthusiasms and shall therefore make no invisible choir of* show tunes or slowly push up their coffin tops and perform Fosse choreography. I know Coco is a huge fan of the "Thriller" video and used to do the entire dance interlude in their kitchen, but she has promised she will refrain from any and all Jackson homages once dead and buried.

There will no playing ultimate Frisbee with their halos, pulling down dandelions by their roots, or haunting calls from their horizontal phone booths to the teens who visit the cemetery to swap spit (and more). The Kopelmans are also not the type to play femur field hockey, with or without baby skulls as the balls and your mausoleums as goals. You have my word as a public official that when they kick the habit of oxygen, their dirt naps will be the apex of serenity for your community, which, while now six feet under, was high society in their days of breathing.

Many thanks for your consideration, Mr. Morash.

Secretary of State John Forbes Kerry

THINGS I LIE AWAKE THINKING ABOUT AT 3:14 AM

SANSA STARK CAN'T GET A FUCKING BREAK

How is Sansa Stark doing?

That "November Rain" video was so epic.

Is Aunt Jemima married to Uncle Ben?

Where is Joe Pesci these days?

Why do I enjoy getting drunk and taunting Siri so much?

Why is it called Ruth's Chris Steak House?

It's so funny to call an asshole a chocolate starfish.

Valextra sounds less like a luxury handbag company and more like a prescription dick pill.

I hate "video art."

Is the plural of *doofus doofuses* or *doofii*?

I wonder how much a three-bed in Dorne would cost me?

Thumb wrestling kind of just went away.

How is dead editor Diana Vreeland coming out with a perfume?

After all these Canada Goose jackets, are there any geese left up there?

You know it's a movie when the girl has her hair covering the rubber band part of her ponytail holder.

The composer of the 1-877-KARS-4-KIDS jingle should be mangled by wild boars.

1- 877-KARS-4-KIDS = 🙁💦

Hozier is so hot even before you hear the Irish accent. Dzamn.

"Baby, It's Cold Outside" is actually so rapey.

Why is the face in the Kumon logo so displeased?

Has anyone ever seen Ke$ha and Iggy Azalea at the same time?

Why does stuff taste better on long thin spoons?

Candy corn: I don't get it.

Why don't these people get that their spray tans make them look like Tony the Tiger?

There is a special place in hell for people who tickle your stomach while you're stretching.

I wonder if there's a new dying-teenager movie opening this weekend.

Does every community have a furniture seller with really lousy homemade commercials starring family members?

Why are there still ventriloquists?

Watermelon gazpacho is not gazpacho.

Someone should open a *fromagerie* called Cheeses Christ.

Someone should open a sake bar called For Christ's Sake.

Someone should open a Japanese fusion restaurant called Miso Hungry.

Someone should open up a salon called Curl Up and Dye.

Someone should open up a bread shop called House of Carbs.

Why do office buildings have keys to the bathrooms? Do they think we're gonna steal cheap TP?

Rene Russo—Where she at? She was so iconic and breathtaking in *The Thomas Crown Affair* and became my aging role model. I need her to resurface so I can have a glimmer of hope that you can still be sexy at sixty.

Who exactly is buying those snot-colored cars?

What exactly is a flying fuck?

ARIE'S WORDS TO LIVE BY

My hilarious dad, Arie Kopelman, is, at this writing, seventy-seven years old. A true comedic genius who can do any accent and countless shticks, he is part Borscht Belt, part Chris Rock. (Incidentally, he is Rock's number one fan and was in the audience for an HBO special and the camera has him exiting over the credits saying, "Fabulous!") During his years at Columbia Business School he tried his hand at stand-up on the weekends, with occasional gigs in Atlantic City and Reno. When he told his parents that he'd been secretly nursing this goofy passion, his father—a very cerebral, laconic judge who acted like he was on the bench even when the robe was off and the gavel put away—replied, "One word: disinheritance." My dad jokes there wasn't exactly anything to inherit, but he got the picture immediately and abandoned the comedic stage, only to go on to have an incredible career in advertising and as an executive at Chanel, where he was president for twenty-five years. He has a great work ethic, he's a strong leader and a truly imaginative thinker, but I believe it was his humor that fueled his ascent in the corporate world. He still calls Chanel's owner to share dirty jokes (the latest involving old men in nursing homes angling for hand jobs from the old ladies with Parkinson's) or hilarious anecdotes (the latest involving heinously rude clients), and all his friends—professional and personal—say his perfect timing and unparalleled ear for accents are as good as any professional comedian's or impersonator's.

Lucky for my brother, Willie, and me, Dad has laced sage advice with his famous humor, his version of a spoonful of sugar to help the medicine go down. Here is a sampling of a few key winners—instant classics, I think—that Willie and I adore.

"If you stir shit, it smells worse."

Indeed. This gem has come up at a kajillion points in my life and I have shared it with my own kids. Have a fight with a pal that's all apologized for and settled? Let it lie. Annoyed by something that you'd like to get off your chest? Don't be an idiot—zip that cock washer.

As part of the life's-too-short category of wisdom, my dad believes that while sometimes we need to express our feelings, sometimes unburdening yourself becomes a burden to another, like tossing an emotional grenade. If there is, in fact, a desperate need, go for it. But always measure consequences before picking at an emotional scab. Example: You hear some beeyotch said something about you and entertain the fantasy of going up to her and asking WTF. Then it's a whole confrontational bloodbath. What's the point? What do you gain? Never let them see you sweat. Don't stir shit.

"You can't dance at two weddings with one tuchas."

Slow down. Breathe in and out. Be present. We hear this a lot, but I prefer my father's way less-wellnessy, woo-woo way of saying it. I've had several moments in my life when my ambitions got the best of me and I've run myself ragged. Workwise, schedulewise, running around in a stressed fog. The nadir was when I had three kids in three schools. I was schlepping all over the city and never stopping to rest and I got sick and didn't get better; and my dad said I was *too skinny*. Which was shocking because he's kind of a fattist; he unashamedly loves thinness. Not like Donald Trump or anything—he's never said anything mean or used the word *pig*—but he has made it clear that he takes issue with gluttony in general. Trying to give the benefit of the doubt to all, my mom has been known to try to defend the people my dad is judging for their portliness ("Oh, Arie, maybe it's glandular!"). But he is quick to chalk extra weight up to "open pieholes in search of seconds." So I was floored when he commented I was too skeletorious. I burst into tears, saying I was tearing all over the city nonstop, juggling so much; and that, at the age of thirty-five, I was completely drowning in my life. I told him I was just one group playdate away from having a full-on Tony Soprano–style panic attack. He instructed me to scale back and stay focused, learn how to say no—no to charity committees, no to being class mom, even no to parties sometimes—because one can do only so much.

Breakthrough! It was tremendously liberating; now I don't even make excuses, I just say I can't do it, sorry. So when you feel pulled in countless directions, just stop, stay calm, and choose where you want your *tuchas* to be, and be there.

• • •

"That guy was born on third base."

Sometimes my husband, Harry, gets discouraged by people our age (or younger) buying third homes and flying first class or throwing parties nicer than our wedding just to "celebrate summer!" (Attire: denim 'n' diamonds). Some of these people, of course, have real talent and deserve all their hard-earned success. Others, as Dad would say, "were born on third base," aka "come from the Lucky Sperm Club," aka "had a huge head start with family dough," aka "got beaten with the lucky stick." Said stick is passed around Wall Street a lot and leads to shot-pounding dumb dumbs with luck-begotten private planes saying, "Wheels up!" (Newsflash: "Fire up the bird!" is the new "wheels up." As in: "You guys want a lift to camp visiting day? We're firing up the bird for Portland if you want to fly Air Goldberg!")

lucky sperm club

My friend Henry Cornell is a totally self-made Goldman partner, and he said one of his five kids was complaining about something (as all kids do), and he just said, "Hey, a billion kids just woke up on a dirt floor." That's something my dad would say. He values hard work above all else and always reminds us never to aspire to the trappings of what seems like a glamorous life. All that glitters is not gold and the guy born on third base will never appreciate getting to home plate as much as the one who grinds it out and around those bases or who smacks it out of the park on his own.

"You marry a rich girl, you kiss one ass; you marry a poor girl, you kiss a million."

Another way he put it? "You can make more money under the chuppah in five minutes than fifty years in business!"

You don't know Arie, but if you've been paying attention to the other phrases here, you may rightly be thinking this one doesn't seem to sync with the guy I've been describing above. Stay with me. He has a good point—more an observation about society than actual instructions for me to follow.

My dad said this to me—attributing it to his own grandfather (who may have used it less ironically)—when I was going through the phase of dating messy artist types who lived in total squalor. To be fair, I was just compensating for a nasty breakup with a polished, bespectacled prepster who made me alternately haul ass to his country club on the weekends or rot in the car like a dog while he visited his grandpa in a million-dollar old-age home that for some reason I was not allowed into. I drove the cart while he golfed and I recorded his scores diligently with a dwarf pencil stamped in gold foil with the club logo. After all that lavish greenery and the accompanying manicured country house, a painter's filthy studio apartment with coffee cans filled with color-encrusted brushes somehow seemed super sexy. Picture Yugoslavia in the nineties. But it seemed oddly appealing, like I was playing a role in some abstract expressionist drama full of flinging paint and ruined shirts and the smell of turpentine.

But my dad got it right away. He saw the mental elastic snap I was going through. He knew I was rebelling against something. Relaying his grandfather's line had nothing to do with income—he actually would have loved it if I married someone who had some kind of stable income, no matter the level if he loved what he did—but rather the lifestyle of artistic struggle. He didn't want me paired with someone who was actually into the hand-to-mouth hustle. Still, I have to laugh when I think of the great-grandpa I never knew saying this to him. And though the era of making an "advantageous marriage" is luckily behind us (along with dowries), there will always be a funny unspoken truth about wanting a stable life. But Arie has always had a stern warning for the other extreme, which was even more significant.

"If you marry for money, you earn every penny."

My dad is so morally sound that, while he never would have wanted me to live in squalor or be struggling all my life, he also

I LOVE BUYING SHIT! OH, WAIT.... I HAVE TO FUCK YOU NOW? UGH.

would never want me to be the thing he despises the most: a gold digger. Whenever we saw some crusty old gent—Crypt Keepers, he called them—with a blond cheerleader type on his bony arm, my dad would ask, "Would she be with him if he were a pharmacist in Passaic?" They might be getting into a Ferrari or coming out of Vuitton, laden with glossy, swinging shopping bags, and he'd observe that she might be psyched for a flashy Saturday night, but she had to wake up with him Sunday morning. Oh, and by the way, she had to FUCK HIM. Earn every penny, indeed. Life is too short.

"Success has a thousand fathers and failure is an orphan."

This Arie classic helped me during the years I trolled the lowest rungs of moviemaking development hell, seeking cinematic homes for my novels. Sitting in production offices, you'd think everyone in the place won an Oscar. Every office had framed posters of every imaginable smash-hit film. Scratch the surface and you'd find out that the person whose wall the poster hung on was, like, the gaffer's assistant's brother's roommate or the coffee runner for a backroom executive, but still ... they hung up the poster to latch on to the hit—which is great, because everyone should have pride in their work! The flip side is that if something bombs, everyone is lightning quick to distance themselves—"I didn't have the creative control I wanted"—even if they did work very, very hard on it in a more important way. In other words, people pass the buck on failure but take full credit for success. Don't be fooled.

"Money doesn't care who owns it."

The dentist who invented the tooth implant as we know it. The largest Jacuzzi distributor. The patent owner for temporary tattoos. You name it, there is a fortune behind every invention. And the eight- or nine- or ten-figure bank accounts often don't match the look or taste or poise of the person who holds the checkbook.

Por ejemplo: Imagine a couple making a grand entrance into a restaurant. He's cheesy and in a suit that could have come from the *Sopranos'* costume department. She has a rack that could double as a flotation device if they were to wreck their yacht. He's sweaty and meaty. She's wearing a huge fur coat, a tiny bandage dress, and lots of bling. They sit down and order steaks, and when they come, one of them does what my mom, Coco, calls "playing the cello." This is when, rather than holding a knife and fork like a normal well-mannered person, the person stabs into a steak holding his fork vertically, sawing away with the bow/knife horizontally. I might say, "Uh-oh, Yo-Yo Ma in the house." And Dad will throw out that awesome line.

In late 2015, *The Wall Street Journal* ran an article about Klaus Obermeyer, the now-ninety-six-year-old founder of the Obermeyer ski apparel company. In it, Obermeyer attributed his great and lasting health to his daily workout program. My dad forwarded it to me with the following message:

My program is so much better, which is why I still look like a matinee idol:

1) I spend at least 45 mins on the pot, reading and pooping.
2) I stay as inactive as possible—vegging is a great way to think.
3) I stretch for 45 mins every day—my own Zen.
4) I have fabulous grandchildren to admire and worry about.
5) I read the obits every day. I am grateful for every day I ain't on the list!

THE LIFE - CHANGING
MAGIC OF DOKKA MIFF

Aside from my parents and my mom's gyno, who helped yank me into this crazy-ass world, the first person to hold me, hours old, was Dr. David Smith. As a baby burrito swaddled in my New York Hospital standard-issue blankie and pounding formula, I couldn't have known that the man who checked my vitals under the nursery French-fry warmer would grow to be one of my favorite humans on this blue-green orb we call earth. The most brilliant pediatrician, with the best medical instincts and bedside manner, the man also happens to have a sense of humor that none can rival. He's Woody Allen with a stethoscope.

My mother said that he never failed to crack her up, calming her nerves with funny quips and making even unpleasant visits, which involved booster shots, fun by being so hilarious. Once my brother, Willie, twisted his ankle, and my dad asked Dr. Smith if we should tape it. His response: "Not unless he's starting for the Knicks tonight."

Now, this might sound a little weird, but I went to Dr. Smith

(I repeat: my pediatrician) until I was twenty-four. I just didn't feel comfortable switching and he never made me, so it wasn't until my parents strongly suggested that I switch to their internist that I left Dr. Smith behind. I didn't know it at the time, but my hiatus from him would be short-lived.

I got married when I was twenty-seven and was pregnant one year later. My mom bumped into Dr. Smith's wife and relayed the news of our impending stork visit. "Wonderful! Who is she going to see for a pediatrician?" she asked. My mom mentioned the woman I had tentatively picked (who seemed to be a bit cold to me and kept me waiting forty-five minutes before meeting her for the prospective patient interview).

"Oh, why? She should go to David!"

"I thought he retired!" Mom said, mentally tabulating his age.

Nope, still going strong.

So I called him up and shared the news of my baby's due date and asked if he would be our pediatrician. A few weeks later, Sadie was born and Dr. Smith reentered my life. In the same hospital where he met me the same month twenty-nine years earlier, Dr. Smith held my baby girl.

"She is your grandpatient," I said, hormonal and misty.

His hair was grayer, but he had the same glasses, same New York Hospital white lab coat (a vintage piece, as it had since switched names to New York–Presbyterian Weill Cornell blah, blah, blah), and the same unmistakable booming voice. "Dr. Smith here!" he said as he swept into the room. It was such a joy to see him holding my kid. He met my husband, Harry, and then my parents came in. My mom hugged him. In the years to come I would realize how special and important the pediatrician-mom relationship is. You're in the trenches together. Every fever, stomach bug, vaccine, flu shot, and specialist referral I called about, I'd get that reassuring, superhero response: "Dr. Smith here."

Contrary to my expectations, I was rocked with terrible post-partum depression for about three weeks after Sadie was born. I cried during Volvo commercials. There was one where the mom is picking up her little girl from ice-skating lessons and sees the girl keep falling and spending half the lesson on her butt, so the mom turns on the passenger-seat ass warmer. Bawling.

I am the happiest person I know and never got depressed, even as an angsty teen. But there I was, so elated to have this baby and yet feeling like I had a boulder on my chest every time I woke up. I had no help, which I realize was stupid in retrospect, and I was so sleep deprived I thought I was losing my mind.

"Listen, Jill," Dr. Smith said to me with his forceful veteran's confidence. "Stop trying to be a perfect mother. Try to be a sur-viving mother. If you can do that, you'll be just fine and so will your kids."

He saw me pregnant two more times, coming to meet Ivy and Fletch when they each arrived on the same floor of the same hos-pital.

When Sadie was little, she couldn't pronounce *Dr. Smith* so she said "Dokka Miff." It stuck. The whole Kargman household lovingly called him that, even writing it on his Christmas card. Through the years, Dokka Miff helped me find my sanity on many other occasions:

"Dr. Smith," I sobbed, "Sadie keeps spitting up!"

"Too bad you didn't marry a dry cleaner."

"Dr. Smith, I'm calling from Paris and Sadie has terrible diar-rhea."

"Tell her to lay off the Bordelaise."

"Dr. Smith, Sadie's two and she's still addicted to her pacifier!"

"I've got news for you: She won't go to college with it."

"Dr. Smith, Sadie is almost three and she's still laying cable in her pants!"

"I guarantee she won't walk down the aisle in diapers."

Once, at Ivy's checkup, he measured her height per usual. Ivy stood up as straight as she could, her huge eyes waiting expectantly for news of her growth.

"Ah, thirty-six inches!" he exclaimed. "We can get you a job! We can use you as an exact yardstick. You can work for architects or carpenters or decorators—lots of people need a yardstick."

Later I was so stressed out from the kindergarten admissions process and juggling my two small fries who were born a year apart (oops!) that I broke down bawling in Dr. Smith's office.

Somehow he managed to soothe my frayed nerves, assuring me that I'd be through the swamps of Mordor in a few years and that there was a light at the end of the tunnel.

I can't even count the number of times he calmed me down, talked me off a ledge, and most important, put the kiddies at ease when a needle was coming their way. Not because of the free sticker box under his exam table or the promise of a lollipop post-shot. But because his warmth was so disarming that even the most doctorphobic child grew to love and admire him.

One day a few years ago, I received a letter from the good dokka. After careful and thoughtful deliberation, he had decided to retire. He wrote:

My heart will always be in what has constituted my whole life: taking up the cause of my young patients by helping their parents be the best they can be at one of the most difficult, stressful, but fun jobs on earth. The joy I have derived by sharing in the life of my families has become my personal pleasure. Being able to be a part of their growing up, following their lives from childhood to adulthood and (amazingly) into parenthood has been enormously satisfying. When parents were proud of their children, I was proud with them. When children grew into successful adults it was part of my success as well. What profession could there be that equaled my own?

Tears streamed down my face. My best friend, Vanessa, and her sister Isobel and godsister Virginia and I had an impromptu Reply All email chain which functioned as an Internet support group. We were devastated. He was irreplaceable. So much more than just a physician, he was our wizard of wisdom.

The truth is, kids don't like going to the doctor much, nor do grown-ups, I suppose. But now that I'm in the normal healthcare system—a factory with rotating nurses and a flash of lab coat for ten minutes and no more old-school office chats long after the blood-pressure squeezie thing has been put away—I appreciate Dokka Miff all that much more. I long for that precious time of human connection that he gave me and my kids. In a youth-obsessed culture and city where everyone wants the new, new thing, he was the exception to the rule.

FIVE THINGS I'D TELL THE TEEN ME

1. It is total bullshit that "these are the best years of your life."

They're *so not*! Being young is great in many ways, but it's not the peak of life, so don't let anyone make you feel "lucky" to be young. Adolescence is filled with stress and frustration and waiting to be free. Also, there's the one-chance-only pressure of applying to college, which sucks balls, but the hardest part is getting in; after that I promise you can chill a little. And then there's getting dumped. That bites, but there will be others who won't dump you (you might dump them) and someday, perhaps, someone you can count on. Being a teenager blows and it will get better. Swear.

2. Zits clear.

I had bad acne and had to take a prescription to help clear it up. So I know that zits suck and that there's almost nothing that will make you feel better when you've got a full-on Mount Vesuvius on your forehead. But I really would have liked to know that when I got older it would all clear. And that I wouldn't have to deal with stressful to-pop-or-not-to-pop questions or applying cover-up with a sponge. It's really unfair that during the most emotionally tempestuous time of our lives Mother Nature throws down cystic acne to complicate matters. Twisted bitch. But maybe she does it to help us hone our personalities and learn not to coast on looks. Maybe it's character building and the only way to appreciate our clear skin later. I know I do.

3. You have not yet met all your bridesmaids.

Friendships are tricky when you bond at a young age, because oftentimes it's simply proximity or inertia, geography or geography class throwing you together. But one day soon you will find friends who seem to have led parallel lives. You will develop lingo instantly with these kindred spirits; you'll complete each other's sentences. And there is a safety in those sisterhoods unlike the catty crap of high school. I had only two extremely close friends I could trust in high school, and that's plenty. And if you don't have them yet, you will.

4. It's so good that you didn't drink.

Guess what—those hot blond girls doing keg stands? I have news for you: They peaked at sixteen. Would you want to be your best self in eleventh grade? Fuck no! While perfectly cool with bobbing ponytails at the time, those party girls all look like crap now. They fried on the beach in bikinis with Panama Jack, they pounded shots to stay in with the guys, they smoked. At forty-one, when I see some of those girls from my past, I can't get over how hagitosis maximus they have become. Granted, I have armies of crow's-feet marching out from the corners of my eyes, but from laughter, not excessive hard alcohol, ciggies, and sunburns.

5. Love is on the way.

Drawn hearts in the notebook margin and romantic stories in your head will one day feel real instead of fantasy. Just hold on tight. There will be douchebags and loneliness and longing so painful you will feel like you will barf up your heart, but be patient and, most of all, be your own unedited kooky-ass self. If you make your quirky path interesting, with all its twists and turns and "Billie Jean"–style light-up steps and grooves, inevitably someone will come along and want to walk it beside you.

BONUS! Johnny Dynell and Chi Chi Valenti will deejay your wedding.

When I was underage, I used to get all decked out and sneak into bars and clubs with my wide-eyed seventeen-year-old pals, not to drink but just to dance and people watch. One of my favorite clubs was called Jackie 60. I was obsessed with the husband-and-wife deejay duo Johnny Dynell and Chi Chi Valenti, and little did I know that a decade later they'd deejay at my wedding. Not one person wasn't dancing their ass off. It remains one of the best parties I've ever been to and it was supremely cool to have them at the turntables.

ORLANDON'T

My friends began teasing me the second I let the cat (or, ahem, *mouse*) out of the bag: I would be taking the plunge and taking my kids to Disney World, which I call Misney World. I'd been saying for years that Fletch needed to be out of diapers, but his days of laying pipe in his shorts had come and gone and we still hadn't, well, gone.

I know I was not cut out for the Happiest Place on Earth. I went as a child, full of wonder and excitement, but the rounded-corner, matte photos I still have from that trip tell the truth. The faded brights of Floridian sunshine are a-splash on my seventies clothes. My little brother looks semidisturbed in the embrace of a giant furry monster. His face is a straight-line smile, half grin, half grimace. His expression embodied my apprehensions about this trip as a parent, too. There's a reason I call the place Misney World, after all. As in Misery and Disney.

First of all, there is the exorbitant price tag. Just getting there and getting tickets for the parks costs the same as the Ritz, Paris.

Swear! And then there is the fact that I HATE THE SUN and Florida proudly calls itself the Sunshine State. I think they should change that license plate slogan to Land of Humidity and Sunburns. I knew my locks would frizz to Cuba, I would have pubes sprouting from my head the second I stepped off the plane.

But cost and vanity aside, as a mom of three kids under six, I was more or less paralyzed by the fear of losing a kiddo in the crowds. I'd heard the story of a former head of the FBI who was poached by Diz to become their chief of security after a nugget-snatching incident where someone shaved a girl's head and put her in pants, trying smuggle her out as a boy. The perv got caught but, uh, nightmare!

"Think about it," my friend Konstantin said, when I told him how shocked I was by the horror story. "That place must be like Costco for child molesters."

Great.

And then there's the people. I'm not a total misanthrope, but the type of people who flock to Disney make me one. Example: Disney honeymooners. What twisted, sick, fucked-up couple would want to go *there* for their honeymoon?! Well, tons, apparently. It's the number one honeymoon destination in America. I almost plotzed when I heard that. "Oh, baby, yes, *yes*, do me with those Mickey Mouse ears on! Oooooooh, baby, take me Pluto-style!" Dassome messed-up fucked-up shizzle right there.

More messed-up Mickey-related truths:

Getting there: The crazy vibe begins long before you get to the phallic-shaped swing state itself. The departure lounge at your local airport will be an odious sea of mullets awaiting the boarding call. Children will be in tank tops in fifty-degree New York

weather and parents will be sporting iron-on T-shirts in that vel-
veteen eighties font that say the family name and "Annual Disney
Trip!"

I would "guesstimate" that 20 to 30 percent of our flight's
population had custom-printed T-shirts for the occasion. One
couple had "Jionni and Jenni's 1st Anniversary"! (*Note:* that hor-
rendisssimi spelling, not *Gianni* or *Johnny,* but *Jionni.* That should
be some kind of misdemeanor). Custom *annual shirts?* Annual anniversary trips? In my book it was "one and done"—a check in
the box that I'd accomplished my mission. I would take my litter,
make the photo book like my mom had, and *basta.* My friend Ra-
chel said, "Jill, it's like childbirth—it's excruciating but you have
to do it once per kid." But she is a better mom than I am. I guess
I had Disney triplets because I informed all my kids this was a
one-time thing—no Kargman Annual Trip shirts would be or-
dered with the year on the sleeve. This would be *it.*

The colors: When we arrived, the color scheme immediately
changed. My New York City grays and browns were eclipsed by
coral and teal. Florida is made up of tertiary color wheel hues.
Salmon. Magenta. Tampon box designs. And skimpy! A teal bra
with a coral cami over it then skin, skin, skin. So confusing. Snoo-
kis on parade. In the sea of feet with bright toenails or worse—
the omnipresent French pedicure with white strip and, naturally,
toe rings—I spied a guy with a nice Northeastern-looking bur-
gundy and yellow striped university scarf. A preppy! Ahhh, a
modicum of comfort. Some familiarity! Finally, someone like me
who perhaps maybe even went to boarding school! We could exchange eye rolls and bond! I edged closer to him, and his university scarf, wouldn't you know, was the scarf for Gryffindor.

Awesomeness. As the weekend continued, any stitch of even remotely academic-looking gear I saw was Hogwarts issued.

The prefab accommodations: We stayed at the Grand Floridian, but it should really be called the Mediocre Floridian. The carved marble inlay of Goofy heads in the lobby were mildly amusing, but for the staggering price, we could have gone to any Relais & Châteaux and it would've been *much* cheaper. At least I hoped the room would be palatial for the price.

No such luck. The joint had a beige plastic bathtub from twenty years ago, and the ersatz colonial décor was enough to make you start itching right away. Harry pretty instantly forgave our normal Hotel Rule (if you're paying for an expensive hotel room, you have to have sex in it), because Ariel from *The Little Mermaid* could be heard singing her "ahhhhhh" out our window and that's just plain box drying.

"Um, I'm sorry, is it me, or is everyone here contest winners?" I asked my husband, looking around at the toothless meth-head clientele.

"Oh no, not at all," Harry replied. "I had complete sticker shock at the rates and I asked our travel agent what the fuck, and she said people save up for years and expect to spend about five months of salary on this trip. They take second mortgages out on their homes!"

You could've knocked me over with a feather plucked from Donald Duck's duff.

No wonder Main Street is broke! Shockingly though, that was only the beginning. You know that Keyser Söze gimp Kevin Spacey line: "The greatest trick the devil ever pulled was convincing the world he didn't exist"?

Well, he does. And he doesn't wear Prada.
He wears a Mickey Mouse–trademarked T-shirt.

The maddening merch: I know I shouldn't have been really surprised, but I was and so just have to comment: the never-ending glut of merchandise/shit at Disney World could fill an ocean that even Jack Sparrow couldn't plow through. From the moment we arrived until the moment we left, we were beaten over the head with the opportunity to buy more crap. Every spinning teacup or whirling coaster or other dizzying vomitfest dumps you out into a gift shop hawking loot so you'll never forget your hellacious odyssey.

And then the pins. Early on, Denny—our Akron, Ohio, born-and-bred Welcome Guide—explained that the Disney pin system was a trading currency, like cigarettes in jail (my interpretation, not his).

Each of my kids was given a new pin (the patented safety backings of which were rubber Mickey heads, natch) and was told they could buy more at the M. Mouse Mercantile on the second floor. Then they could trade with people from all over the world around the parks. The pins could be worn on clothes or a lanyard, which was like a credentials holder, covered in Made in China–stamped Ariels or Beasts or Nemos.

And thus began the obsession with collection pins. Everywhere we went my kids wanted to stop and trade and buy and trade and buy. Oh, and BTW, each POS pin featuring a character head ranged from seven to twelve clams apiece, not including the Rare Collectibles kept in special glass cases. Every time another parent slapped down plastic for a commemorative pin, it was gasoline on the flames for my three. All they wanted was pins. Sebastian the crab. A midriff-baring Jasmine. Jack Skellington (which I caved over because I love him). They cried tears over these pieces of junk! Fletch approached a paralyzed kid and requested a trade for a Spider-Man pin (attached to the kid's pin-covered wheel-chair), and I was so mortified I wished my wrist could shoot a huge web over him and fling him back to the shitty hotel room.

The stupid-ass pennies: In addition to the pin craze, Denny also suggested we might want to purchase a (Made in Vietnam— perhaps by an eleven-year-old) smashed-penny album.

The smashed-penny machines are ubiquitous around the hotel, the monorail, and all the theme parks. The smashed-penny machine allows you to commemorate your ride by inserting four quarters (*and* providing your own penny!), then pressing a but-ton. The metal works of the machine crank away and then shit out your copper, now oblong and with Buzz Lightyear beaten into it. Awesome. The albums—which come in a colorful array of options and premium versions featuring every Disney character imaginable—have enough slots for fifty ovals. So, in addition to buying the expensive albums, you now have a holder for $50.50 worth of copper turds.

The only good thing about the Happiest Place on Earth is that I slept like the dead. Probably because that's how my soul felt. Though each morning I woke up ravenous.

The food: Which brings me to the food. Or rather, lack thereof. Unless you want kielbasa fingers and a ring circumference the size of a Hula-Hoop, you simply can't eat there. Funnel cakes and French fries abound; a "small" ice cream is enough to choke both

Ben and Jerry. Though, alas, it's not their brand, but rather some chemical goop that even I, the least farm-to-table/seed-to-anus obsessed person ever, could not stomach. And then there is the theme park's trademark item of sustenance, perhaps the most shocking thing of all: the gargantuan bacon-smelling turkey legs. People

GIGANTIC POULTRY

walk around carrying these enormous drumsticks that make them look like Captain Caveman, dining on mutton. It's like the fucking Flintstones in there. Except instead of one-shouldered cheetah togas, they're sporting wifebeaters, frattoos of Psi Pi Alpha Sigma Epsilon, and hats with Goofy ears dangling off. We're talking about grown-ups here FYI. One guy *my age* was chowing a huge turkey leg with a Yoda strapped to his back. He chucked the bone *on the ground* and it almost hit Sadie in the fore-head. But most people made the effort to at least dispose of the carnage in the appropriate waste receptacle. I once looked into a trash can and there was just a *mountain* of bones. Every single day at Disney World is like a turkey holocaust that dwarfs Thanks-giving. Piles upon *piles* of leg bones. The. Nastiest. Thing. Ever.

The lines (and the solution to them that makes you feel ter-rible): I'm *so not a cutter*. I believe in lines. But the average wait at Disney World (on a good day) is two hours. Two hours standing there and then four minutes on the ride itself. What a complete waste of time.

Sure, you can get a FastPass+ and cut the wait down to a half hour or forty-five minutes, but the ratio of waiting to riding still blows. Everyone I knew said that the solution was to hire a guide, a person who will gladly take your money to help you get past all the Make-A-Wish kids.

The whole guide racket is a nightmare. I was so upset about the lesson I was teaching my children ("Throw money at someone and you get to skip ahead!"), but the alternative, zigzagging marathon seemed awful, too. So I'm ashamed to say we did it. Our guide was an Australian transplant and he got the equivalent of a litigator's hourly fee for his evil work. But I credit him with saving us from noose roping ourselves. Maybe he even saved my marriage.

The characters: Okay, then in addition to junk on a stick and snack bar food, I was told by everyone that I'm a bad person if I don't take my kids to the "character meals." These made me feel like I was on another planet. Truly. For the right to watch everyone at the table hold hands to pray before eating their chicken stew and rice pilaf (which came from the hair-strewn chafing dishes at the buffet) and the chance to mingle with one of the princesses working the room, you pay sixty clams a head (no matter how small the head; no child discount!). I'm sure Jasmine's and Aurora's and Cinderella's proud families in rural Alabama (wait, isn't that redundant?) tell everyone that little Brianna is in show bidniss. Meanwhile, she's posing for iPhones in a dress others wear for Halloween. Apparently being a princess is one of the most coveted jobs in the area. I guess it beats stripping.

One culinary bright spot on this "vacation" was a place called the California Grill. It was not only not bad but had a full sushi bar, a thrillingly long wine list, and an eclectic menu. They also offered a "maki roll" for dessert: gummy worms (fish) surrounded by Rice Krispies treat (rice) and wrapped in fruit roll-ups (seaweed). With chocolate sauce instead of soy. Aces. Disgusting, but A+ for creativity.

> *One happy moment at the Happiest Place on Earth*
> I'll grudgingly give credit where credit is due: The fireworks were some of the best I've ever seen. My nuggets were awestruck and transfixed, rhapsodizing over each colorful burst of light.

Like the painful Floridian sunshine burned on my retinas, our experience at Disney is burned into my soul. I won't forget it. We won't do it again. Apparently that attitude makes me "not a dreamer" (an actual quote from an Upper-East-Side-by-way-of-Louisiana mom who loves Disney and goes every fucking year).

I'm fine with that. My kids loved the trip, so it was worth the time and money, but I don't think they are desperate to go again. Case in point: When we piled on the shuttle to the Orlando airport, the TVs had a farewell message from Goofy, saying, "See ya next time!" Four-year-old Ivy yelled to the animated dog, *"I don't think so!"* and Harry and I died laughing. Orlandon't, that's for sure! Maybe my nondreamer side has trickled on down and poisoned my children. I'm okay with that, too. 'Cause despite the fireworks, fairies, and balmy weather, the truth is, when I wished upon a star, I wished to be back in New York. There's no place like home.

JEWS IN THE WOODS

When I was nine, my parents decided that I should get out of the Manhattan frying pan and get into the campfire: eight lung-clearing weeks of summer sleepaway camp. I was game. My best friend, Dana, was, too. I know it sounds insane to many, but for East Coast Jewy Jewsteins it was the norm to venture away from the grit and grime of big-city living for that amount of time in rural Shangri-la.

It was also de rigueur to research and find your camp by inviting salespeople to pitch you the merits of their camps in your living room. After narrowing the options down to four, we invited the camp directors to our house for a presentation to both Dana's and my families.

My mom made a platter of cheese and crackers and dips, set out drinks, and turned out the lights. Over the course of the weekend, the directors hooked up their Kodak Carousels and projected the woods of Maine onto a screen propped in the corner. The pictures and narratives told of blissful, hazy summer days and sailboats, tire swings over water, grinning kids on water skis, horseback riding, green fields, and campfire-roasted marshmallows.

Ultimately, choosing would be somewhat of a leap of faith, since all the camps had the same basic elements. We went with the process of camp-director elimination.

Proving that you can both be bald and have split ends (a receding hairline and a long, curly mullet in the back), one director described everything as "the best in the business." The best location in the business. The best staff in the business. The best equipment in the business. After his detailed boast of state-of-the-art dance studios, a theater rivaling those on college campuses, and an allegedly haute cuisine dining hall, he closed his colorful pitch by adding with a wink, "Quite frankly, we are the Rolls-Royce of camps."

He got points for salesmanship and panache; but my father stood up, shook his hand sincerely, and walked him toward the door. "Thank you so much for your time," he said, "but I think we're looking for the Chevy of camps."

Finally, we found our fit in the last of the litter: a mellower, cooler-seeming place with hip-looking counselors (in the slides at least) and less "best in the business" flash. Even with a slide show and home visit, it's still a shot in the dark and an eight-hour bus ride to Maine. The two-month chapter before you can be daunting for a child. I admit I was nervous.

My camp had looked somewhat ramshackle in the presentations but once I arrived, I knew it was a perfect, picturesque spot: perched on a lake with a fleet of rainbow Sunfish boats at the edge, and docks creating a swim area where hot campers plunged daily. There wasn't Instagram then, but the entire spread was very postworthy. There were ceramics, tennis, field sports, archery, rifles, and rocketry—the works. The food was perfectly fine.

I was plenty homesick at first and I wasn't exactly Miss Popular that year. The girls in my bunk all had photos of their dogs—who were named Pepper or Feffer or Steve—and thought it was *superweird* I didn't have one; but I explained that where I lived, one had to pick up the logs with an inside-out Duane Reade bag, which was shocking to them, since they all had yards in Jersey where their mutts could lay cable wherevs. Despite being a city slicker unused to wooded paths, the allergens of cut grass, or the nighttime call of loons, I powered through and found my groove. One of the things that helped me was the camp radio station that we all tuned in to via the tiny and primitive boom boxes we were allowed to have brought from home and could leave on our little cabin shelving unit and turn on quietly at rest hour. The cute older boy deejays introduced us to nonquiet tunes by Quiet Riot, AC/DC, Def Leppard, and we lived for it. I wanted my own show badly.

I chose disc jockey class during free time right away, and by August, I had my very own half-hour slot on the docket. The head deejay/counselor, who worked the switchboard and put me on the hot mic live, was named John. He introduced me to The Cure and The Smiths that summer, music that I still love today. The hut/station was right next to rocketry, so you had a bit of a contrast between the geek-chic, techy, tube-socks next-door set and the Clash T-shirts in the booth. But I loved hanging around in there, perusing vinyl jackets and eavesdropping on the teens about who made out with whom.

And, importantly, I learned to hone my comedic shtick between the songs, making observations about camp and hamming it up on air. Soon campers were coming up to me, letting me know they'd laughed at my silly voices or liked something about my show. In later years, those hours at the mic gave me the confidence to try performing on a stage rather than tucked away in a booth in the woods.

Camp meant smooching with boyfriends on the wooden benches (I later learned that the counselors were instructed to shine a flashlight and break things up "if the bench starts shakin'"), dancing to blaring B-52s at weekly socials, and friendships we would remember forever.

Camp also meant G-rated traditions. We had an annual twenty-four-hour swimathon, an insane two-day color war with a full gauntlet of crazy challenges, field trips to nearby harbor towns, and a carnival with a marriage booth where you could pledge faithfulness with a pipe cleaner ring.

There were also some highly questionable traditions, too. Like the slave auction, the most fucked-up thing ever. Each bunk could earn brownie points by passing inspection or doing chores around camp. A certain level of points won you a golden ticket of some sort—wampum that you could pool with your cabinmates' resources for the main event: the auctioning of counselors to be the camper's slaves. Bonkers. Forget that it was harking back to the horrors of human trafficking and replicating the Stanford prison experiment, but also it taught us that we could have people serve us. As children. All you had to do was pay enough.

The summer I was twelve, my entire bunk was in love with Damian, a water-skiing counselor from England, who we all knew was banging Trish, the blond aerobics teacher. Trish had a white BMW—with vanity plates—that she kept under a sheet in the parking lot. Heinous. I was determined to win his lot, which was listed in the slave catalog as, "Tuck in and Kisses Good Night from Damian." Fuck Trish, he was *mine*! My cabinmates and I worked hard for our golden tickets and worked hard to curry favor with the ticket-dispensing staff: We got bull's-eyes in archery, learned to drop a water ski, and kept our cabin squeaky clean.

The night of the slave auction arrived and Damian's price rose and rose. We knew we had the most, and we won him, crushing our rivals' Damian dreams. We even had enough tickets left over to also win breakfast in bed from some un-hot counselor. But who cares about that. We'd *won Damian*! The night of the visit, we all fried our hair with hair dryers at the same time, blowing a fuse so the lights went out. We primped in our pajamas in anticipation. When he arrived, he sat on my bed, clearly understanding that I was the ringleader/stalker in chief. Oddly, he told us all a beautiful fable of how trees came to be, but his voice was, as Linda Richman would say, "like butta." He then circled the cabin, giving each of us a kiss good night. I practically had to wring out my white elastic-banded Calvins.

Fast-forward twenty-eight years. All three of my kids go to this same camp; Sadie started at the same age I did. Some things have changed.

Gone is the graffiti. That radio station? A fully equipped studio with an ON-AIR red light outside the glass booth. Slave auction? Fuck, no! Now there is metalsmithing. A spin studio. A ropes course and a climbing wall.

The crowd has morphed a bit, too. The current director is

awesome (he was a camper when I was there!), but there has been an explosion of JAPs. Every year at visiting day, the director takes out a bullhorn to welcome the parents at the driveway of the camp as we are all corralled behind a ribbon. After a few details about the day, he snips the ribbon and so begins what is known as *the running of the Jews*. It is Mel Gibson and John Galliano's worst nightmare. Aggressive, loud yentas and helicopter dads in finance sprinting Pamplona-style to get to their little messiahs.

I had gotten a glimpse of a few of these pieces of parenting work at the bus stop in New York when the kids boarded for camp: flat-ironed JAPs with skinny jeans and huge oversized Jackie O shades at 7 A.M. with leashes on four standard poodles and hapless husbands carrying Zabar's foil cold bags onto the bus. As the kids pulled away for Maine, the parents ran after the bus screaming, *"I love you!"* And pointing at their eye, then making a heart over their heart, and pointing at the kids behind the tinted-glass windows, who were busy tearing into their E.A.T. fifteen-dollar smoked salmon panini with the crusts cut off. I heart you, baby! I heart you, you spoiled little creature!

On visiting day I was stunned to see these same parents lined up with Baked by Melissa boxes, Lester's bags, even Shun Lee, because darling Dakota or Jason or Jonah was missing ethnic food. They took private jets up, they schlepped piles of presents for their offspring—from table-size Rice Krispies treats monogrammed with the bunkmates' names to rainbow looms to friendship necklaces for the cabin.

I have to admit I was terrified. Would my daughter come back demanding Fekkai shampoo and mani-pedis? Now she had peers whose parents flew sushi to the boonies for these brats! Fuck. Harry and I were stressed.

As soon as we saw Sadie, I launched into an explanation that echoed what my parents had explained to me: If you get everything, you will have nothing to look forward to; there is an emptiness inside inveterate shoppers and incessant consumers; rungs to be climbed, holes to fill, always; when you feed the beast whatever it wants, it's always hungry.

Maybe we'd taught her well, though. All that bad, pampered, entitled behavior spoke for itself and Sadie seemed to know how *not* to be after exposure to it.

And not all the kids were like that, by a long shot. She found her posse—from what I can tell a bunch of sweet, strong, kindhearted, unspoiled girls. They have photos of themselves with their arms around each other; they whisper jokes, giggle over silly and private camp memories; their eyes sparkle as they recount details of pranks.

Perhaps now it has become the Rolls-Royce of camps. But it still has the soul of a vintage, well-loved Chevy.

WHY I WILL ALWAYS *Love* THE UPPER EAST SIDE

Even our beggars are choosers.

Once I was in line at a Starbucks on Third Avenue and passed a hungry man asking for food. So I went inside and bought him a sandwich. When I came out and handed it to him he said, "Ugh, it's on wheat? I hate wheat."

There is a panhandler who parks his wheelchair outside Viand, the old-school diner catty-corner to Barney's, where people drop

tens of thousands on threads every day. For as long as I can remember, my mother has always given him a few dollars every time she sees him, and I have always tried to do the same. One day recently, I changed things up: I asked him if I could buy him lunch at the diner and, if so, what would he like (lesson learned from the Starbuck's incident). He said yes and proceeded to place his complex order with me: Russian dressing on the side and smoked, *not* roasted turkey, for starters, and then a whole host of fixings.

My yard kicks your yard's ass.

When people move to the suburbs, I take it personally. Their exodus is like a slap in the face.

The main reason most cite for their move is "my kids need a yard" but that reasoning only makes me madder, slaps me harder. Hello! Central Park is the lungs of Manhattan! And it's fucking bigger than any suburban acreage!

My friend Julia diagnosed me with the invented affliction known as SPD: suburban panic disorder. Mostly it's because I can't drive, so I feel marooned when I'm out of the city, but also it's because I live for strolling home after dinner, window-shopping, feeling the electricity of the neighborhood and the life-blood of my work. I always say I'd rather live in a fifth-floor walk-up studio than a mansion in Greenwich. I'd wither on the vine outside my beloved city. Westchester County makes me ask Siri for a tutorial in hara-kiri. Back in the city, my friends and I ask her for instructions on less lethal things, like how to give great blow jobs.

I also resent moves to the suburbs because I know they mean I will never see those friends again; it feels like a breakup. Sure, they all say the same thing: *That's nonsense! We'll be in allll the time! It's only twenty minutes.* Bullshit sneeze. In no universe is it twenty minutes to the city from anywhere. I can't get to the East Village in that time, and you're telling me you're coming over a bridge or winding your way through da Bronx? Maybe in a Ferrari at 3 A.M., *maybe.*

You can feel okay about plastic surgery.

What's a man to give his wife who has just about everything? Now that we're in our fourth decade, new tits seem to be the gift of choice. I'm fine with my own low riders but, like my *Odd Mom Out* character, Jill Weber, I seem to be the designated boob-job chaperone/picker upper. I guess I've become the boob feeler, too: One friend asked me to inspect her "new Hidalgos" (named after the doctor who would do the surgery), the actual synthetic gummies, before they were put into her chest forever.

I recently went to pick up another pal at her melon specialist but she was still passed out when I got there, so I was told I'd have to wait an hour for her to come to. There was a blizzard outside at the time and I didn't want to freeze to death walking around, so I plopped down to read a magazine in the well-appointed waiting room. More interesting than the magazines was a leather-bound tome of the doctor's best work. Because this was not my first waiting room wait, I knew that other plastic surgeons have these as well—the before-and-after schnoz-to-ski-jump noses and low-rider flapjack boobies into pert perfect ones. But this book was different. It showed before-and-after boob/

eye/nose jobs on the one page and then a cleft-palate child in Peru before and Joaquin Phoenix–like scar after! Page after page was boobs, then Operation Smile kids. Streisand-to-Witherspoon nose, then burn victim transformation. This guy was like the Robin Hood of plastic surgery! Park Avenue cans by day, Siamese twin separation by night! Later, I told some friends about this scalpel-clenching superhero, and they used his goodness to convince their husbands to buy them procedures: *See, honey? My new tits are altruism! If you buy me a new rack, a kid in Uruguay will get a new face!*

We've got a joint where everybody knows your name.

Donohue's is a dark mahogany pub and has been serving food (and my favorite turkey sandwich) and drinks for years, unchanged by the commercial explosion along Lexington Avenue. With its old-school German black letter font signage and small window looking into the wooden interior, Donohue's is hiding in plain sight among the flashier, in-your-face eating establishments that have cropped up around it.

It doesn't look like much, but when you go in it's like *Cheers.* Only mostly gay. I can't tell you why, but Donohue's attracts fabulous old queens in their eighties and nineties and their younger Filipino handlers or husbands. But then there's also the "regular" and more familiar crowd: There's Liz Smith the columnist, there's Matt Lauer at the bar with a sandwich. Vanessa Noel the shoe designer has a cot in the back, I think, because she is always there. She's basically the Norm of Donohue's. Everyone is kind and welcoming and there is no scene at all because all the snobbish people are in the fancy restaurants that dot the city and the neighbor-hood.

My family has been obsessed with Donohue's—keeping the secret of its existence mostly private (until now) and eating there whenever we can. It's had some publicity over the years—it once shot to short-lived fame when *The New York Times* wrote about an old gentlemen without heirs who died and left the Donohue's waitresses five-figure tips. It's a cozy sanctuary, and in the winter its toasty interior and welcoming warmth are better than any fireplace at home.

It gives me material like shooting fish in a barrel.

People ask me all the time if I ever get scared I could run out of material for *Odd Mom Out,* and I have to laugh. Fuck, no! I have ears and eyeballs, remember? The surroundings, the people, the world I inhabit (albeit mostly on the un-chic fringes) can yield twenty seasons of humorous plot lines without trying. Whether it's the balloon lip injections or conspicuous consumption or banker husbands talking about their $250,000 McLarens (the cars, not to be confused with the differently spelled strollers), it never ends. We've got the Israeli movers who will allegedly bang you for an extra fee. And the people who argue earnestly over whether Glamsquad or Vênsette is the better in-home, before-event makeup and hairstyling service. The women who say they're fat after half a tuna tartare. We've got stomach stapling. And elite pet kennels, where you can live-stream spy on your cat's spa treatments. The wacky OTT hyperbolized petri dish is the gift that keeps on giving.

WHY I WANT TO DRESS FOREVER YOUNG

You know when you and your friends spy someone who just exudes Rock Star? You crane your necks in a crowded restaurant or hopping bar and go, *Who* is *that?* Sometimes it's an actual, aging, weatherworn bassist, but often it's . . . a civilian. A nobody who just *looks* like a somebody. A guy who may be regular but still somehow evokes throttling strings, pounding drums, and grazing groupies. But why exactly? What are those magic telltale pieces that smack of, well, *smack,* but also the sexy power of a larger-than-life, grinding guitar god?

Part of it is definitely the clothes. The postapocalyptic, hyperstylized, *Blade Runner* look gives a guy a tough, dark, gritty vibe. Testosterone has something to do with it, too. But thank goodness for Joan Jett and other female badasses. After all, as Joan sang in "Bad Reputation," "A girl can do what she wants to do." And what is rock 'n' roll about but rebellion?

. . .

When I turned forty, I decided I was not going to put myself out
to fashion pasture. Yes, I'd cut my hair at thirty-five, but not
because some beauty magazine told me to. Fact is, there are
some looks that women *d'un certain âge* should not rock. I go
nuts when I'm walking behind someone and observe her long
teenage ponytail or miniskirt or hooker shoes, only to find at the
crosswalk when I am next to her that she is the Crypt Keeper.

I chopped my hair because it was fried, dyed, and pushed aside.
But after the cut (of about eight inches), I worried I looked like a
newscaster and went into compensation mode. I bought investment

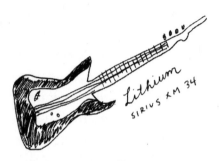

"pieces" (sorry, I hate when
people call an item of cloth-
ing a piece, but they were)
and never bought the trend,
only my vroom-vroom vam-
pire look.

Because to me, rocker
chic never goes out of style.
Female "recording artists" these days make my skin crawl. You
can have the nasal girlie squeals of the annual, inevitable on-
slaught of cheery "songs of summer." The Barbied-out pop tarts
have infused the red carpet with spray-on Day-Glo neons and
have—to quote Patsy from *Absolutely Fabulous*—"hemlines so
high, the whole world's your gynecologist."

But there's another way. Is that a revving motorcycle engine I
hear? Could it be a razor-sharp edge emerging in the sea of fluffy
cotton-candy pink? Rick Owens, take me away! I'll be your backseat Betty anytime.

I like to think that as long as my hemlines are appropriate and
the clothes aren't too tight, I can rock a rock 'n' roll look to match

my attitude. It's who I have always been and I'm not growing out of it, even when I'm seventy.

In the thicket of pop soda-pop that makes my ears bleed, people continue to Debbie Downer me and pronounce that rock is, in fact, dead. But as Nirvana alum Dave Grohl once explained at the Grammys, rock 'n' roll is doing just fine, thank you very much, as demonstrated by his Foo Fighters' category win for an album cut literally in his garage. Granted, there probably are four Porsches parked in there, but still. Better than the legions of cheesy-ass femmebots dying their hair the colors of Easter eggs to get attention.

There are some of us—as much as we try to steep ourselves in pop culture and therefore pop fashion—who simply fiend for the Trash and Vaudeville vibe of good ol' cymbal-smashing, face-melting, go-home-with-the-waitress rock 'n' roll. In my novel *The Rock Star in Seat 3A*, the main character, Hazel, is a just-one-of-the-guys-type, potty-mouthed, heavy metal–blaring chick who works at a video game company. While I myself am decidedly way more feminine, her scorching affair with her throaty-voiced rock idol plunges her right into the world she (and I) always fantasized about.

And clearly others have, too. The excitement of blue lights hitting rising smoke as the fevered crowd roars has held an allure for everyone ever since the first concert front man cleared his throat at a mic. Or hers. MTV disseminated that look when I came of age, and there appears to be a nostalgia now that we are hags and harking back to our younger days of headbanging yore. One example, aside from iconic ol'-school acts mounting major tours (think: the Big Four's multiband sellout at Yankee Stadium), is the success of productions that take place in that smoky backstage milieu. *Rock of Ages* is, to my family, a cult classic of sorts, and I continue to hold out hope (or a lighter!) that people will rekindle their love for stadium rock—the late-eighties answer to the lipsticked synthfest from the middle of that decade (of which I'm admittedly also a fan). The Los Angeles scene certainly had the girls who put the *strip* in Sunset Strip, flaunting torn fishnets with cleave- and booty-baring skintight numbers. But the new rock 'n' roll has a delicious androgyny to it—now the gals can rock Slash's leather jacket. And I do. Who cares if I'm older or a mom or not in a band. It tells the world I'm not going to rot in pleat-front JCPenney mom jeans complete with tapestry vest, per the *SNL* fauxmercial for Mom Jeans. My penchant for rock style isn't about the male rockers and the women dressed as their clingy sluts—now we can rock the ensembles ourselves, and in a chic, equally badass way. There is a bubbling up of the black-and-silver combo, from super-skinny suits to killer violent boots that scream "check check" at the mic. Women can now rack up a wrist full of Chrome Hearts thick chains that were once only found in the men's section. Even fine jewelry has taken a vroom-vroom twist with goth rhodium everywhere—charcoal metal making you want to come on and feel the noise just looking at it. And it appears that black diamonds may be hard rock's answer to rap's D-color bling (ironically). Tons of designers are now adding subtle onyx bling to graphite metals for an anyone-got-a-guitar-pick? vibe. Bolder belt buckles are back, their carved sterling harking to countless unzipped flies of those sex, drugs, and rock 'n' roll years. While healthier living has been embraced and many people have purged the sins of the era, there is still a way to travel back stylewise in a more refined, tailored way, but with the same violent-but-sexy spirit as before. So feel free to eschew the bubblegum hues and choose something that would make Ms. Jett proud. Put another dime in the jukebox, baby, and don't be afraid to trade in that Lululemon for a Straight to Hell buffalo hide motorcycle jacket. And while the glossies may pronounce lime green or lavender a hue of the month on the rainbow-encompassing runways, for me, the limited spectrum will always be charcoal to black.

QUESTIONS FOR THE COSMOS

Artisanal: The word is *omni*! Who needs fennel-seed-dusted handmade organic rolls? Just gimme some bread, yo.

WOULD YOU LIKE TO SAMPLE MY $24 ARTISINAL PICKLES? THEY'RE SEED-TO-ANUS.

Cheese pizza: Redundant. Like saying assless chaps.

Black Friday: Where did this come from?! Since when was hitting Target on par with the tramplings at Altamont?

Dog strollers: Make it stop. When I was little, dogs were on leashes and kids were in strollers. Now kids are on leashes and dogs are in strollers.

Easy listening: More like difficult listening. I've said for years that only serial killers listen to that garbage and was totally vindicated when the *Girl with the Dragon Tattoo* movie showed Stellan Skarsgård entering his rape/slaughter chamber and blaring Enya.

Fur vests: If it's cold enough for fur, then why would you want your arms out? [Also see: "Awky fall hooves," page 198, and please reconsider knee-high boots with an open toe.] Useless.

Meteorologists: Do they call people who study meteors weather-ologists?! Also, PS, I think it's amusing when Al Roker says, "Here's what's happening in your neck o' the woods" and tosses the broadcast to a local weatherman. The local guy always chuckles and says, "Thanks, Al." I want to yell *What do you mean— thanks, Al?!* Roker couldn't pick you out of a police lineup and you're all on-air chummy like he just sent his camera right over to you, Shane Blaylock of WKTV, Pocatello, Idaho!

WALKER WITH
TENNIS BALLS

Old people's walkers with tennis balls: I'm sorry, but can someone *finally* please invent walkers that come with some kind of antislip base? Plenty of perfectly innocent Wilsons are being slashed across the throat and shoved on the bottoms of walkers. And too many grown children and grandchildren are accidentally slashing their palms open trying to cut the tennis balls open in the first place.

Plate bowls: They make soup cold so quickly! I like a fucking deep-ass bowl of soup, not some shallow plate masquerading as a bowl where my thimbleful of soup gets cold in seven seconds. There. I feel much better getting that one in particular off my chest.

"Sale! 10% off!": Don't even fucking bother. Ten percent off is not worth the walk to the boutique; sales tax puts that fucking 10 percent right back on!

Stick figure decals of your family on your car's back window: I thought they were the most depressing things in the universe (we don't care to know the exact makeup of your fucking family!) . . . until I saw a stick figure family with Mickey ears on it. See "Orlandon't" if you even have to ask.

Another time I saw a mom and three kids, and clearly someone used a razor blade to scrape off Dad, who had a piece of shoe left. He must've put his stick dick into another tennis racket–toting mom decal. Much more amusing, but I still don't care!

Wires that hold down my son's action figures in the box: Did we make some pact with China to punish parents for their impatient kids or something? Why should it take ten minutes to free a fucking toy from its packaging? Spider-Man can scale tall buildings and survive his shipment from Asia, but I need garden shears to set him loose in Manhattan. Too annoying, this packaging.

FOREVER SISTERS

ONE DAY GERTIE
WILL MARRY
YOUR BROTHER

When my hilarious, gorgeous brother moved to Los Angeles weeks after his college graduation, I knew he'd slay. He had told me that the famous movie producer Louis B. Mayer once sent a friend "back East" a letter that said something along the lines of *It's great here: The women are knockouts and your only competition is a bunch of idiots.* Willie would have his pick!

As a protective and suspicious-of-Hollywood older sister, I forbade him (in vain) to date anyone with a head shot in her purse. That lasted about five minutes, because they were everywhere he looked. They were "actresses" whose claim to fame was playing a toe-tagged dead body on a gurney on *CSI*, or they were bartenders who wanted to be models, or massage therapists who wanted to be models and actresses. You know how every four years at your high school there is a legendary beauty everyone talks about? Well, *alllll* those girls across the whole country move to LA with stars in their eyes. And many of them were smitten with my charming brother.

For the record, Willie is not a modelizer—he is super down-to-earth, values brains over bods, and has a fierce wit he'd like you to keep up with. The hardest laughter of my life has been by his side. So, no, he is not a model chaser—they chased him! And what dude with a dick would say no?

But he chose monogamy. Always. He sought deep relationships and never was a banger playboy; he stayed faithful to the same girl for months or years; he tried to make things work. Which is the good news. The bad news was that in his attempts to take things seriously, he brought every girlfriend home to meet the family at holidays. In the summertime it was particularly challenging because they'd be prancing by my husband in a white string bikini while I was obesifying during a cankle and thankle pregnancy, but at least in later years they helped with my babies and toddler. They wanted to impress, so it was nice having a free au pair of sorts, even if their hemlines were way too short for my parents' country club or my taste. Or ego.

I made Willie swear after each breakup that that would be the last person with an 8 x 10 glossy. Eventually he sought out a higher-caliber woman: there were writers, fashionable editors, smart girls with cool careers. Then one day he told me he met another actress. *Ugh.* Setback! I rolled my eyes—not again—they're all insecure, on-the-make climbers!

Then he told me her name: Drew Barrymore.

Wait, what?!

I was excited, because naturally I loved her the way all of America loves her, and wanted to hear every detail—was she as sweet as she seemed? What was he going to give her for her birthday that she didn't already have? When would we meet?

After two months, Willie introduced her over dinner in Santa Monica. I walked in kinda nervous for obvi/surreal reasons, but she stood up and engulfed me in a huge hug. I melted. I was immediately disarmed by her warmth, her sparkling eyes, and the radiating friendliness that you get from her on the screen. And, most important, I'd never seen my brother happier. The months passed blissfully for them and I felt totally comfortable with her, though I sometimes worried about overtexting (I am a certified emoji addict) and maintaining her privacy. For example, would it be weird to send her a picture of my kids on an *E.T.* ride? Ask her about ex-boyfriends the way you would with a normal friend even though I knew they were famous actors? Questions about movies she was in? Which celebs were nice and who were assholes?

You know how women in Jane Austen novels never talk about becoming sisters-in-law? They go right to "We're going to be sisters!" That's how it is for Drew and me. And is she ever astute about Kopelman family patterns: She once commented that the average was seventeen minutes before someone at the dinner table brought up death. She is a delightful happy mirror to our familial morose dark side, and the perfect yin-yang of California sunny outlooks versus our wintry dark humor. At home she is makeup free, casual, cooking meals for my nieces, singing kooky songs, rocking out with a funny dance to make them laugh. Slap on some red lipstick and a dress, though, and you're like, *Whoa, mom to movie star in five minutes!* She can foxify in record time, and when we leave the house, people spaz over her. She gets mauled by strangers, weeping and begging for selfies. There's something about her that engenders a feeling of closeness from fans. Maybe it's because we all watched her grow up—from beloved little Gertie to producer powerhouse to beauty empire entrepreneur— and have cheered her on at a distance.

Drew's real best friends, unlike those of many actresses, are not all famous. Cammy D (aka Cameron Diaz) is an exception. One Christmas, she stayed with us for a week, and when I was sitting with the two of them, drinking wine, I imagined myself morphing Asian into Lucy Liu and picking up guns and tearing shit *up*. Super fun fantasy.

One day during her stay, Fletch busted rudely into Cam's room and found her naked. Unfazed, he asked her which of the two Matchbox cars he was holding was cooler. She picked the red one and he said thanks and wheeled for the door. Just before he exited, he turned to her and said suavely, "I'm five years old." We died laughing when she told us. My son lived out every male fantasy and somehow knew it as a kindergartner.

Sometimes when one of Drew's movies is on TV, I rewatch it and, yes, it feels slightly weird to me that I've plopped on the couch and eaten crap food with the girl on the screen playing Cindefuckinrella. Even though she and Willie went splitsville just as this book was going to print, we are forever sisters. Bottom line: She is a Technicolor flower child bouquet of a person, and a welcome kaleidoscope of hues that infused our Addams Family with optimism and light.

THINGS THAT TOTALLY
M. NIGHT SHYAMALAN
ME OUT

Automatic toilet flushers: Dear makers of these things: Sometimes we are *not ready* to flush! I know you invented the autoflusher so peeps don't have to touch the handle, but, come on, that's what feet are for. And anyway I'd rather have to wash my hands than get a pee-splashed butt.

ATMs that slurp in your card rather than having you swipe: I love a good Citibank card dip. When I go to some creepy alternate banks and they deep-throat my card, I fear that it will (a) come out shredded, (b) never come out ever again, or (c) I will get my cash and walk off, leaving it in there for all eternity. I really wish all were the dippy kind.

Children in leopard leggings: JonBenét was the first household name for the toddlers 'n' tiaras looking-sexy set, but now it's all gone too far. Little girls are four-going-on-whore more than ever, and dat shit ain't riiiight.

Cilantro: IMHO, the devil himself. And dill is his bitch. People always thought I was weird when I asked if any dish had cilantro, and then I found vindication in a *Times* article saying there was genetic hatred of the herb passed down in DNA. I knew it!

American Girl dolls: I'm scared they will come to life and stab me to death if I don't buy them more accessories and shrunken out-fits. Sometimes I think Ivy's twinsie doll has the run of the house when we are on vacation.

Going over the Visa bill with my husband: Nothing, and I mean *nothing*, dries up a pussy faster than going over the credit card statement. Line by motherfuckin' line.

HARRY

ME

Can we go over the VISA bill?

NOoo oo o oo. !

Headbands that look like a braid of hair: Disturbing. Ditto ponytail holders that are scrunchies made of fake hair.

Identical twins who are dressed alike: I'm sorry. I know people think it's cute and everything—and maybe for babies and toddlers it can be—but somewhere at around five it starts to look a little *redrum*-y. Also, I'm no kiddie shrink, but aren't we supposed to encourage individual identity? Isn't it better to be your own self rather than someone's Diane Arbus–y doppelgänger?

Lazy Susans: Now, I think of myself as a pretty generous soul. But two words I hate together? *Family style.* When I go out to dinner with a group, and some dictator decides they're ordering for the table and we will all partake in *sharing* by swiveling our dishes on this hellish round beeyotch, I want to explode. My one beloved dish is inevitably at noon to my 6 P.M., and by the time it swirls around, there is one sad pan-seared dumpling left. Susan, stop being so lazy! Get off your fat ass.

Keebler Elves campaign: This series of commercials from my youth seemed normal at the time, but now I find it super creepsville that these tiny, tree-dwelling Aryan Smurfs had their shrunken paws all over my fucking cookies.

The massive rodent problem in that rich family's house in The Nutcracker: You people are having a blowout Christmas party with a staff of ten and the kids are wearing silk and opening life-size dolls. Can't you afford an exterminator for the *teeming* rats cruising your living room? No one thinks of this. I see that ballet every year and I'm so grossed out by the hordes of rodentia in this rural Austrian mansion. Maybe they don't notice the droppings around that mammoth tree? Unclear. And very upsetting.

Men eating bananas: I'm so immature, but it just looks so blowjobby! Women eating them doesn't, for some reason that is beyond me. Maybe it's because I think of women as healthier breakfast eaters, while dudes have a breakfast burrito or egg sandwich with sausage and cheese. In fact, come to think of it, I don't really like men eating fruit in general. Don't be so vain! That's our thing!

'Rexifur: In other words, when skinny girls (size 0) have enough hair on their arms to clog the drain with one arm shave with a Gillette Mach3.

People who hold the mug from the not-handle side: I can't take it. There's a handle for good reason! Somehow this habit smacks of smugness, like those people in a coffee commercial, sipping by a fire and discussing prose.

"Take a chill pill, Jill": People who say that need to jump off a cliff. I have been hyper since I was born. I know I have a lot of energy. But I am not high on cocaine (I've been accused of that several times). On occasion I do ingest a Xanax to soothe my fried nerves, but when *I think* I need to. Keep your suggestions to yourself!

Tapas bars: Yes, I know they're trendy and somehow cool. But (a) I despise the phrase *small plates* (I'm *hungry* and also hate family style) and (b) it always sounds like *topless bar*! Without fail, when someone is saying they're going to a tapas bar, I just think of greased boobs and girls jiggling their way through nursing school. I personally think it's high time someone open a chainlet called Topless Tapas! Like Hooters but with better food and with stripper poles. Oh, and big portions! We could serve stuff like quesaDDillas and margari-tatas. Instant success.

Tom Cruise's middle tooth: My friend Konstantin pointed out that while most of us have two front teeth, Tom Cruise has three. Or one, I guess. Once you see it, you cannot unsee it. Look directly beneath his "angel press" (the divot under your nose that meets your lip, so called, as I was told when I was a kid, because an angel put its finger there when you left heaven to say shh). It's so bizarre. Google dat shit, you'll pee. If you just search for "Tom Cruise middle," the tooth pops up. I still show friends and cry laughing at the images. It's more fun than getting drunk and taunting Siri.

Waiters who don't write shit down: I'm sorry, you may be an actor trying to hone your memorization skills, but you stress my shit out. Inevitably the order gets fucked up and arrives with unwanted lardons, and all you had to do was get a fucking pad and a pen. I mean, really, do you think peeps're like *Oh my! All that food is in his head, let's leave a 40 percent tip!* Not happening.

Pick my brain: You're just asking to harvest a few tips from me, but all I can think of is Hannibal Lecter sawing at the top of Ray Liotta's skull, flipping it open like a can of Campbell's soup, and sautéing cerebellum chunks with garlic butter. Call me crazy, but I don't really feel the need to take time out of my schedule or away from my family to let you do that. Talk about hemorrhaging time.

Journey: Unless you are talking about the band, please shut up. Talking about your life's "journey" smacks of SoCal cheesiness and spiritual gangsta narcissism. Or of wandering in the desert where the air is so hot it squiggles in the distance and you lose your mind and start talking to cacti and then when you eventually make it home you won't shut up about your Life Lessons. As they said in the nineties, "Tell it to the hand." Or as I say, "Tell it to the wrist 'cause the hand is pissed."

Pet peeve: I have so many pet peeves that the actual words *pet peeve* are a pet peeve.

Roman numeral names: Shakespeare taught us many lessons, one of them being do not name your son after yourself. I am all for tradition, but this one blows, as I have personally seen people either rest on their laurels or collapse under the pressure of Daddy's name. The way I see it, Roman numeral I sows it, II grows it, III blows it. IV and V, well, that's just obnoxious at that point. To quote *Sex and the City*, "The higher the number, the worse the sex." Or as I say, the higher the number, the smaller the dick.

ALL HAIL TURKEY DAY! 🍴

Thanksgiving is my kinda holiday: all food, no religion. Since my family elevates eating to an art, it's fun to have a day that toasts not just the American stuffing of one's gullet but the actual process, the smell of the food cooking, the setting of the table, the Norman Rockwell presentation of Tom the Turkey. When I was young, we stayed in New York City for the festivities, sometimes crossing the park to watch enormous Garfield and Smurfs float by. Inflatable Snoopys are a far cry from Indians sharing corn, but, hey, Matt Lauer commenting while Dora the Explorer's butt is behind him has become its own tradition.

When I hit high school, my parents got a house in Massachusetts, the original home of the Pilgrims, so we began the pilgrimage (so to speak) up there for our feast. Suddenly I felt so much more enmeshed in the vibe: flickering lanterns lined Nantucket's quaint Main Street and our boots walked over hand-placed cobblestones rather than cement city sidewalks. The air crackled with the smell of the fire in our fireplace. The orange flames created a visual warmth, too, against the Tim Burtony cobalt fog that rolled through the tiny winding streets of antique houses. Those years were so special because I chowed like an animal and slept like a bum.

But then ... it was time to grow up. I got married and had a child, and travel became difficult, so we were back to balloon mode on Central Park West. My mom cooked every ounce of food, even though my dad, brother, and I begged her to supplement with some store-bought butternut squash soup or Zabar's stuffing rather than taking it all on herself. But no. She had to hand grind the chestnuts and roast the pumpkin and create everything just right. And it was ambrosia. Every year. I popped out two more nuggets so I could help in the kitchen even less. I felt guilty but I didn't want my kids to smash shit in their apartment, so I was on wrangler and doodie duty while my mom did all the hard work.

Four years ago, the pendulum swung in the opposite direction. My brother and Drew were living in Los Angeles with their little kids, and couldn't fly as easily as we could with our preteens and teenager. So we tried a new tradition: the California Thanksgiving. It sounds surreal, and it was, 'cause gone were the chilly winds and early nightfall that justify all that comfort food. Instead, it was all palm trees and blinding sunshine. It's not exactly that hunker-down vibe, stoking fires and chowing sweet potato soup, but it's a lovely reminder that the backdrop is merely a superficial construct and that family around that table is what it's all about. And now that I'm an adult I understand that the perfect, eager faces of that Rockwell iconic illustration are only that—an illustration. The real thing has fidgety kids, squeaky baby toys, and spilled cranberry sauce. And whether your family is blood related or a circle of friends, whether you watch football or parades or old movies, it's a sublime bubble of a day where you don't have to do anything (unless you're cooking!). We have a tradition where we all go around and say what we are thankful for, and this year I'm more grateful than ever to have moments to press the pause button and just float. Like a giant SpongeBob hovering over the park I love.

GLOSSARY OF NEW TERMS

Chico's roulette: A game to be played solitaire (in your mind) or with friends (out loud) in front of storefronts like Chico's or Ann Taylor Loft. The window displays are so damn hid, you force yourself or your friend to pick which outfit you'd wear if there were a gun to your head.

Ghost of fat past: When someone is thin but used to be obe and you just can't forget it. Ex: *He can get super skinny, but I'm always gonna be haunted by his ghost of fat past.*

Real estate boner: When you see a living space that is so amazing you get turned on. Ex: *Whenever I walk between Ninth and Thirteenth streets between Fifth and Sixth avenues and peer into those townhouses, I get such a real estate boner.*

Trip treat: Fellatio at the wheel. Sometimes known as a road job. Ex: *OMG, I totally heard that dad in Greenwich crashed his car 'cause he was getting a trip treat from his kid's teacher.* Never do this. I mean, while the car is moving.

TRIP TREAT

The zacklies: Massive, unbearable halitosis worthy of gas masks. A case of the zacklies is *when yo' breath smells zackly like yo' ass.*

Zach Galifiknock-offs: Heavyset hipster men with thick beards who are so psyched to finally have a cool and hilarious patron saint. Often spotted in Williamsburg or at seed-to-table circle-jerk microbrewery-type establishments.

WHAT A DIFFERENCE A YEAR MAKES

HARRY   ME

I spent my wedding night with Russell Crowe.

Harry and I had just "consummated" (gag) the marriage. I gag at the terminology there, not the act. Because it's not that I didn't want to—*I did!* But isn't there some medieval edict that says you have to bang and seal the deal? Isn't that just whatcha do? I know no one would show up, asking to see the flag-of-Japan bedsheet—proof, had I been a virgin, that we'd gotten busy—in order to wave it in the town square, but I felt the need to start the marriage off on the right foot. So we dealt with our exhaustion and focused on the candlelit dream wedding we'd just been through and . . . got that out of the way.

Allegedly, it's male biology to pass out after sex (and/or after a whirlwind night of partying and promises), and Harry was no exception, leaving me staring at the ceiling, playing the night's twinkling, romantic moments in my head. I looked down at my hand, manicured and decked out with new ice. I looked like someone chopped off the hand of some older lady and glued it to my wrist stump. Surreal.

So there I was, wide awake, with the remote control. Flip, flip . . . home shopping, flip, flip . . . *Full House*, flip, flip . . . *Gladiator. Bingo.* I lay back and somehow this hundredth viewing was so much more emotional. A welling sadness rose within my chest until I burst into tears with full-on audible sobs. They fucking *killed his kid*? And *raped his wife and fucking told him about it*?! I wanted to bash Joaquin's harelippy face in. And this was before he got all psycho on *Letterman.* There was no way someone could be *that* talented an actor and master evil so perfectly without actually being the apex of douchebaggery in real life (at least that's what they all said about Brenda on *90210* back in the day: beeyotch on screen, satanic in life). By the time Russell bites it to allegedly join his dead fam in A Better Place, I was a rocking snotball of a mess.

I'm big on high-budget Hollywood flicks—extra credit for period shit—but the jeering crowds in the Colosseum coaxed some kind of new sadness out of me and a golf ball–size lump into my throat. Why was I being such a drama queen, so hysterical? Was I channeling my own crossing over—marriage means a new chapter, after all—and letting the swirling amorphous sea of my own feelings bubble over into a reaction to Russell's tragic journey? I was so, so, so elated to be married to Harry. And yet I have to admit that I felt a slight melancholy about flushing my maiden name, Kopelman. I had agreed I'd gladly take his name, Kargman—I wanted the same name as my future litter of little nuggets. I didn't know why now I was a lip quiverer; for crying out loud, it wasn't some whole new identity with fifty unpronounceable consonants jammed together or something! It was the same Jewy-Jewstein vibe and identical towel initials and notepaper monogram—*JK*. It was almost the exact same name, just with the *opel* swapped out for *arg*. Not a BFD. I was more than thrilled to see Alison, my so-seventies middle moniker, swirl down the bowl forever, but my last-name change somehow felt like I was leaving my parents behind. I decided I couldn't lie there in bed. I got up and walked through the long marble hallway of my Jay Z suite.

Did I mention the Jay Z suite? Let me back up.

The day before the wedding, I'd checked into the St. Regis hotel, where my parents were married in 1971. We were having a smaller, less fancy wedding, but wanted to stay there for good vibes, since their marriage is so strong and they spent their wedding night there after rolling down from the ballroom. The room I was brought to had a nice setup—one bedroom and a little living room area so that my bridesmaids could get their makeup done while we all sipped some champers from room service before the big event. After the rehearsal dinner, a few of my gals and my gay BFF, Trip, came over to tuck me in. We had a drink and hugged and they left at about 2 A.M., so we could all get down to a little beauty rest.

I turned out the lights, and as I started to melt into the zillion-thread-count sheets and yummy hotel pillowfest, I heard a loud scratching sound from the wall. Someone trying to get in or out? No, I'm a New Yorker and I knew that sound. It was very clearly some hair ball moving around in the wall. Great. Really great.

I called downstairs and tried to calmly explain, in the most antibridezilla, pleasant voice I could conjure, that I was very sorry to bother them, but there was *beclawed rodentia burrowing* near me and did I mention that *I was getting married tomorrow and needed to sleep*? They sent up a dude, who calmly put his ear to the wall, listened to the mystery menace, and casually walked to the phone and dialed downstairs.

"Yeah, hi, we got a code eleven."

No clue what that was, but I inferred from his tone it was approaching DEFCON 1. I wondered, Is that the technical term for *Emergency, this lady is about to lose her shit and we are about to get a Yelp review saying we are infested?*

The next thing I knew, three butlers in tails (à la morning coats, not wall rats) carried all my belongings—including my wedding dress, which was stuffed with tissue paper and stiff like a dead body—to my new room: the Fifth Avenue Imperial Suite. The joint would have made the late great Michael Jackson (and his entourage of nannies, kids, handlers, and the Elephant Man's bones) gasp. It was insane. Ten rooms, a sprawling marble kitchen, a dining table for twelve, a bed fit for a princess (1,000 thread-count bedding, enormous headboard, ten thousand pillows, the works), and a gilded rococo writing desk worthy of signing bills into laws with a quill pen. Score!

So back to the wedding night, where we left me wandering the grand suite alone. I walked to the desk and opened the drawers, retrieving a piece of engraved, watermarked hotel stationery. I sat down to write.

Dear Mom and Dad, I began.

My tears flowed into the ink as I thanked them for the most enchanting of weddings. It was all so ethereal and sublime— during my toast of gratitude on the dance floor I had morphed into Halle Berry at the Oscars: moved beyond measure and sporting mascara cataracts. I know I was not a blactress breaking boundaries. I was just a bride. Who loved everyone in the room.

I wrote them that even though my name was changing, nothing else would. I would always be their BG (baby girl). I wept for twenty minutes straight until I signed *dotter* (tradition). And then something happened. I stopped crying. I folded the paper into thirds and stuck it in the envelope and, as I sealed it, I also closed the flap on my worries. I was Mrs. Harry Kargman now. And I was so glad.

Neither Russell nor the lump in my throat returned. The next few months brought bliss and some travels—first our honeymoon in Italy and then ten days in Tokyo, a business trip for Harry's work that I managed to tag along on by pitching a travel magazine piece on Tokyo's then up-and-coming Cat Street.

Gone for good were my qualms about my name change; I loved seeing *Kargman* on my passport. I loved us being a unit. It was as if our first three months of marriage had shampoo-bottle-simple directions: Eat. Drink. Have sex. Sleep late. Repeat.

We settled in. We enjoyed fun dinners with friends and many weekends away for other people's weddings, which always seemed to reinforce our vows and make us reminisce about our own ceremony. Harry was working round the clock, but I was busy as well, and we were cocooned in a sweet bubble of self-indulgence and fun times, grinning with a newlywed glow.

And then one day I was sitting by the computer, when I started to feel my boobs like . . . buzzing. I put my hands on my chest and m'knockers felt tender and firmer than usual. Like all unsuspecting, head-in-the-sand, potential moms-to-be, I figured I was PMSing.

And then it suddenly dawned on me . . . Oh boy . . .

. . . or girl!

I ran downstairs and over to Zitomer's Department Store

(read: glorified pharmacy, but I love it anyway) with my heart pounding like a timpani played by a cracked-out six-year-old. There they were: the pregnancy tests. How many times had I passed them by and idly thought how loaded the decision to buy one must be. You're either praying for a yes or bargaining with the devil for a no. What did I want?

I bought First Response because they had the most commercials, so their media buyer won my arm-reach to their product. I paid the cashier with what I'm sure was a weird face on, like the smiley face with a squiggly line for a mouth like it might barf. I went upstairs and pulled down the Calvins and peed on the stick. Leaving the stick in my stream for five seconds was gross, but okay, done. Then the instruction said to give it a couple of minutes to marinate in pee. I decided to rest it on the cappy thing it came in and paced in the hall. After two minutes I busted back in and there it was, clear as a nose job on a Horace Mann girl: two pink lines. Holy shit. Knocked up. Bun in the oven. Casting my own Mini-Me. Child star waiting in the green womb. *With child* (how archaic).

Despite that positive sign screaming at me like the Bat signal in the Gotham night sky, I went back down to Zitomer's and bought three more tests, all different brands. As my bladder is roughly the size of a lima bean, there's always pee at the ready. I dropped trou and covered the three tips. *Shwing! Shwing! Shwing!* All three pos. I thought I was going to explode. I didn't know what to do. So I put my coat back on, and went back to Zitomer's. The cashier must've thought I was a recent escapee from the loony bin.

This time to the kids' "department" (read: shelves). I looked at the shrunken clothes and footie pajamas and diapers and bottles and was reeling. Then I spied two tiny booties with lions on them. My jaw dropped. Eureka! Because of his fluffy mane of curly hair, I'd begun calling Harry LC, for Lion Cub, back when we had first started dating. And here I was, with a tinier cub in my tummy. I bought the booties and had them gift wrapped. This time the cashier gave a slight smile, knowing the pee had yielded plus signs. And then I sauntered home and paced, waiting for my Big Lion Cub to come home.

When he texted me he was out of the subway and walking back to our apartment, I couldn't contain myself. I ran down the block and met him on the corner. He looked surprised to see me, especially since I was holding a bow-covered box.

"Hi! What're you doing here? What's this?" he asked.

"Open it!"

It had originally crossed my mind that I could put all the various pregnancy tests in a box with ribbon to tell him that way, but sanity prevailed—it was grody and creepsville to hand him my urine.

His eyes widened as he pulled the booties out.

"NO!"

"Yes!"

We hadn't been trying to get pregnant. But if you must know, we were lazy asses, so it wasn't a total shock. I wasn't into jimmy jackets and neither was he. I called the condies—even his allegedly imperceptible lambskin ones—raincoats. So we bagged whenever I was riding the crimson wave. Or had just finished it. Or didn't feel like schlepping with a boner to the drawer to rifle through it for a dickhat.

"I guess it's true, that joke . . ." I said.

"What joke?" he asked.

"Do you know what they call people who use the withdrawal method?"

"What?"

"Parents."

So there we were on the corner of Seventy-sixth and Park, coming to grips with the fact that we would be parents. And that I would grow to be a fatty. We were both twenty-eight, and while I was lying like a beached whale on the couch eating Ben & Jerry's, my friends were dancing on tables at Bungalow 8. While they were primping in size 4 dresses for a night on the town, I was watching the circumference of my thighs expand by the day. Them: Barneys. Me: Buy Buy Baby.

In other words, Harry and I immediately felt plunged from one club—nightclub—to another club—married folk—and then into the new clubhouse world of parenthood. We had to learn the new lingo, which I have to admit I resented just a bit: Bumbos and Diaper Genies and all this crap we supposedly *needed.* I looked at the airplane hangar–size hateful baby store and asked Harry what the fuck our parents did without all this crap. The way everyone talked about these special bottles and organic this and that, you'd think it was a miracle people survived in other eras.

I started to panic when I went to the baby shower of a fancy-pants acquaintance and all these women were talking about nursery schools and parenting books. I wasn't going to read fucking parenting books! Snooze! What, was I supposed to cancel my *Vogue* subscription and sign up for *Family Circle* now? No fucking way! I started to worry that my identity might get funneled into the fetus. I didn't want to be all about that.

And I had other fears, too. Vag stretching during childbirth, for one thing. And morning sickness made me scared, too. For several months I puked my brains out every day. And for a while there, I felt as if I had taken three Ambiens in the morning! Exhaustion.

But I soldiered on, as women everywhere do. In the end, as my belly got bigger and our first anniversary approached, I realized my pregnancy really helped us nest and was a fire under my (fat) ass to really make a home. Soon we would be a family, and I couldn't defer dealing with the Crate and Barrel explosion that was my bachelorette pad, so we signed a lease on a fourth-floor walk-up and painted the baby's room yellow, since we had decided not to know the sex. Now I look back and feel like a weirdo because I hate when people don't find out! I want to buy them cute dresses or boy shit. (Notice how I didn't say pink or blue? I'm so free of gender stereotypes!) But we stayed in the dark until the baby hit the light of the hospital room.

Before the baby was born, we decided to get away for our anniversary. Harry surprised me with a weekend at a hotel in the Berkshires, the hotel where we'd gotten engaged. We holed up and I got a prenatal massage and we ate like pigs and slept like the dead. After our first night, we told the manager how much fun we'd had and that maybe we'd make it an annual family tradition.

"I'm afraid that won't be possible," he said, looking at my swollen tummy. "There are no children under ten allowed." Ah, okay, another club we wouldn't be allowed into!

Oh well.

The next night, our actual anniversary, I ate so much I felt like I was preggo with twins—my actual nugget and the food baby. What a difference a year makes. My wedding night felt both five minutes and five years ago. So much had gone down. And it was amazing to imagine what the next year would bring. Now we've been together sixteen years and those days seem like eons ago. And while I obviously miss certain aspects like higher T&A and fewer crow's-feet marching around my peepers, I'd never go back. In fact, if you offered me a DeLorean time machine with Michael J. Fox himself at the wheel, I'd take a pass. Such wonderful times lay ahead of me that first year, but also some of the most challenging and exhausting.

Sometimes people say they're waiting a few years to have kids to "enjoy their alone time." Diff'rent strokes for diff'rent folks, but I'm glad I shat out the progeny when I did, 'cause now we're through the tantrum and diaper weeds, and I may be old, but I'm so elated to be on the other side of my own gladiator days of new motherhood.

FUN WITH EUPHEMISMS!

"Gourmet deli" = deli

"Nightlife impresario" = douchebag

"I hate drama!!!" = I love drama!!!

The *Hobbit* film trilogy = *Lord of the Rings* film trilogy but with eye broccoli

"Vintage chic" = dead people's clothes

"Cleansing bar" = soap

"Market price" = You're fucked.

Sofía Vergara = the Charo of our generation

"Tzammy" = how all people named Tammy pronounce it

An enormous polo pony on your shirt = asshole

"At participating McDonald's restaurants" = restaurants?!

"Twentysomething" = twenty-nine

"How was your weekend?" = I don't care how your weekend was.

"Gluten-free baked goods" = main ingredient: cardboard

"Take care!" = Fuck off!

"Acoustic Soundgarden" = sex with a condom

"We're avid art collectors" = We're loaded.

"No pressure" = pressure

"I like functional but still want to have pizzazz!" = wearer of Toms shoes, glitter version

"Price upon request"= You can't afford it.

"No MSG!" = extra MSG

"Post no bills" = Post bills.

"Creative differences" = Someone was an asshole.

"There's a lid for every pot" = Two ugly people got married.

"I'm in a great space right now" = I'm more fucked-up than ever.

"We know the baby's sex but are not telling anyone" = We are annoying.

"Separate checks" = separate beds

"Certified preowned" = used

"Thanks, it was my grandmother's" = *This bling be real, bitch!*

THE VALOR OF PALLOR:
my personal rejection of suntans

I'm the opposite of Natalie Portman's Nina Sayers. I'm no Princess Odette. I'm a black swan dying to become white. Especially as the mercury rises.

me on a beach

As many people know, I hate summer. All the motorcycle-chic black leather that my inner backseat Betty is yearning to wear is inappropriate until the fall. Everyone else embraces bold patterns that look like an FTD truck exploded, but I want to draw the blinds, curl up into a ball, and pray for September. I mean, how many fashion magazine layouts have you seen with the headline "Prints Charming"? I'm itching from the pollen already.

But what to do for my Morticia self come July's heat waves that leave me sizzling on New York's pavement? What do you sport when bold blooms just aren't *you*? How do you get relief when your head is pounding from all the fashion pages filled with looks that suggest all the world's designers looked to Crayola for summer inspiration?

Last summer I looked around and noticed all these frothy pale confections and had a bizarre new urge to pour some sugar on me. Since I obviously wasn't gonna go neon, I went with white. Let the other gals rock the whole yellow-is-the-new-orange citrusfest; in summer, when my goth garb is rendered a shvitzfest, I must adjust appropriately. I don't want to look like a total Cullen for three months, for crying out loud. So rather than turning to candy-hued ROYGBIV spectrum highlights, I hit the ivory coast.

My friends and family said: Huh? Have you kidnapped our Sicilian widow? Are you some alien impersonator?

I know. For someone known for almost militantly wearing mostly all-black ensembles, white may seem like the opposite of my fashion aesthetic. But it ain't actually—that would be, say, oh, I don't know ... coral. The devil. Chartreuse. Gasp! Some hideoso-bright horror show. I can't even tell you what teal does to me. You know how they say the opposite of love isn't hate but indifference? For me it's like that with color. The opposite of black isn't white, it's bright.

Now, many peeps dodge the doily for fear of looking cadaverous, or worse, like Fatty McSorley. But I think that is a myth. White doesn't necessarily make you look wide. I mean, yes, some ladies go bride-orexic for the Big Day, but that's because those photos will live on pianos and mantels until tombstone time (or divorce settlement), and not just because it's white. Matrimony makes us all models for a day.

I personally miss the hell out of my wedding dress. It was the first time I ever felt great in white, and it's lying stuffed with tissue in the Chanel coffin it came in sixteen years ago. I'd love to exhume it and feel that pure again. In fact, other women have told me they feel the exact same way, so I'm dying to have a huge black-tie party one day where we all wear our wedding dresses. It can be like Truman Capote's ball but with veils and rice.

Not that I was, ahem, lily-white in that sense (read: slut bride). Just kidding, Harry! Virgin all the way! Well, would you believe off-white?

Now, with three kids I often shy away from powder-pure blank slates, as these tend to attract a chocolate paw print square on the boob. But for nights out, I might take the Santeria priestess plunge and delve into summer white. There's something so clean, crisp, and fresh feeling about it.

Personally I dig the innocence of a flower eyelet or sweet lacy confection, but some of my pals think those motifs a snooze and asexual, too. But I disagree—they can be white-hot! I mean, doesn't every guy have a sexy nurse fantasy? It's the ultimate in naughty meets nice! Does anyone else remember that Tom Ford tight number with the metal horse thingy detail? A scorcher! Granted, I could never wear that one. Which is why I usually fear white.

White is often thought of as a color for tanned people or sun-kissed blondes; it could be accused of making people like me look washed out. But to that I say, so what? Powder me geisha and wash the shit outta me! Your hair and eyes pop even more when your skin and outfit blend; I think alabaster skin and white look great together! I say, this isn't Rio de Janeiro, the globe hasn't heated up that much, so embrace your SPF'd face by drawing attention to it even more! There is a valor to pallor.

Maybe everyone else will be tricked out in trend du jour fluoro shocking pieces, but fashion's fickle movements aren't edicts and I'd feel way more washed out in acid tones (despite my wistfulness for my Fiorucci neon-pink socks in the eighties) than I do in plain Jane pearl. And unlike the new "it" colors that replace each other like Kleenexes popping out of the box, white is evergreen. Timeless. Forever. And BTW, if the thought of white brings to mind frothy tulle or lace, you can always Kazimir Malevich yourself and go with a minimalist, stark, geometric version that's more cool and utilitarian than sweet and romantic in shape. And if none of these options suit you and all these ideas still don't appeal, take a deep breath and cross off the calendar's gridded days like a prisoner and do what I do: Get psyched for Labor Day.

DID YOU KNOW...

Victoria's Secret is that she had seventeen abortions?

You're allowed to have natural childbirth and not tell everyone?

There are still babies born named Monica?

Mimes will scream if you beat them?

Real estate ads are over-forty pornos?

My dad still calls it a television set?

AT&T stands for ass, twat, and taint?

A red Ferrari is a great way to show the world you're an asshole?

It's totally okay to be edgy and love rock but also Toto's "Africa"?

French vanilla is the same as regular vanilla but with a superiority complex?

The number one cause of unwanted pregnancy is stupidity?

CROCKET, TUBBS, and KOPELMAN

As a die-hard, born-and-bred New Yorker, I'm often asked how it is that I managed to circumvent a druggie phase, the assumption being that drugs grow on or are sold on every Manhattan corner. (They aren't, but they are easy enough to spot anyway!) I have a simple two-word answer: *Miami Vice.* You could not draw a straighter line from drugs to death and destruction than I ♡ DON JOHNSON that show drew for viewers every Friday night in the 1980s. Drug usage always led to a spray of bullets and a chalk outline in a dark alley. "You see," my dad would warn, his eyes glinting through his professorial tortoise-shell glasses, "drugs ruin lives!" We got the message. But we loved watching the mess they made anyway. On TV.

But as much as *Miami Vice* helped steer me clear of drugs and addiction, it also led me down a path toward a short-lived personal style I have to admit to. For all my present devotion to black and an occasional summer white, I did have a mid-eighties color explosion, and *Miami Vice* is to blame.

To my family, it was more than just a TV show, it was a religion. The weekly cautionary tales spun an aqua-kissed underworld that beckoned to my tween self from the blizzards of freezing Manhattan. Everything was sun-drenched and sexy, with leggy, bronzed women dirty dancing against seemingly powerful kingpins or tough cops going deep undercover. It was a sultry style manual of the times. We were told the baby-oiled, Helios-kissed glow was healthy, which we now know put the lie in jai alai.

So there I was: pale, raven haired, and closer to the Central Casting for *The Munsters* than for *Miami Vice*. But I was ten. My brother was seven. And as Glenn Frey crooned, the heat was on. Willie requested a white blazer. I sported neon. Duran Duran blared through the apartment and the "Rio" video echoed the *Vice* look, featuring the same wind-whipped hair and boating odysseys. I went to school on a rain-splattered public bus wearing a drab uniform. *How I longed for a tight turquoise Band-Aid dress!* I was obsessed. And boobies. Everywhere. My classmates called me "flat plains of America" till I sprang swollen mosquito bites at fourteen, so I had an almost lesbianic obsession with the coppery cleavs the women showed off in their white spray-on spandex.

Most Jews say the eleventh commandment is Thou Shalt Order Chinese Food on Sundays, but we moved it to Friday nights for *Vice* viewings. While we cracked our fortune cookies in snowy New York, I could clearly see the futures of those lowlifes trying to outfox Crockett and Tubbs, cruel fates bloodily sealed in machine-gun shoot-outs by the docks, the same ominous music in the background. When the final title, "Created by Michael Mann," appeared as the scene faded to black, so did the goosebumps, followed by a beat of silence (*respeck*!) and then an enthusiastic eruption by my family.

A couple years into our cult-level addiction, my little brother, Willie, who is blond and blue-eyed, was spotted by a casting agent in line at the movie theater. She immediately put him in a toy commercial and subsequently sent him on an audition to play the little son of Don Johnson (i.e., the Messiah) on the show we all worshipped. We were plotzing. I prayed on a stack of Zagat guides he would land the role. He had four callbacks and eventually lost the part, but it was a true pulse-pounding couple of weeks for the Kopelman clan—by then the show had reached its zenith.

But what goes up must eventually come down. Right as I was coming of age. I was starting to be allowed to take the train down to Astor Place and soon discovered the store Trash and Vaudeville. I bought my first black leather motorcycle jacket at twelve, and my inner Morticia stayed for life. As much as I had wanted to be the fuchsia-bikini-clad surfer chick, that simply was the opposite of who I was; between my Kabuki complexion and macabre humor and Tim Burton obsession, I abandoned the kaleidoscopic Kool-Aid for black coffee. I slowly jettisoned any lingering Miami dreams and embraced my own budding goth girl. I started to wear exclusively jet, yielding my mom's nickname for me, the Sicilian Widow. I got my ears double pierced and got a pyramid-spike belt on King's Road on my first trip to London. I was done with the glowing, sparkly hues of Revlon Silver City Pink and on to crimson lips. And here on the dark side I remain, clad almost exclusively in neutrals, wearing brights the last two decades only when coerced as a bridesmaid, and looking thoroughly exhumed from the grave every time.

Naturally, now twenty-twenty hindsight reveals to me that the colors that beckoned on the hit show—many unfortunate pairings of teal, turquoise, and salmon—look more like the hues on a tampon box than something I'd want to adorn my body. What I cherished as sultry from vintage Bain de Soleil ads, I now see as tanorexia, and no matter what side of the law you were on, there was an inherent douchebaggery to the eighties Miami style. Morticia's animal likeness would be a black cat, a raven, a jaguar. Not a fucking flamingo. After all, despite whatever trendy colors weave their way down the runway, black always cycles back. You can't say the same about men's espadrilles.

NOT TO BE TRUSTED

People in teal cars

Of all the colors, *why* pick teal? It has to be linked to mental illness, or else a lack of taste so extreme the driver thinks it's actually cool to reject the norm. When I see teal cars, I always look in the window and, sure enough, there are other telltale signs of instability: rabbit's feet, nose-pick booger-smear, bad music blaring—without fail.

Satan/seitan worshippers

To me, the latter is the former. I mean, if you want to be a vegan, go for it! No one is stopping you! But do you have to preach about it all the time? I am one of the biggest Smiths fanatics ever, but after I saw Morrissey last year and he spent more time ranting about plant-based diets than singing, I decided my fandom was through. I'll still blare the records but don't need to shell it out for a love concert with footage of slaughterhouses in the background.

People who say "My baby is twenty-six months"

No, she's not. I'm so sorry. *She's fucking two.* Just say two, okay? Can't you guys just round up or down? Maybe people feel the need to say their babies' age in months to create a perfect yardstick to measure their progress versus other babies', so you know how awesome they are: They're twenty-three months and not even two and so verbal. Who knows? I always just said the age in years or said "She'll be two in July." Who wants to start doing math, dividing everything by twelve? The winner was a mom who told me her kid was thirty-four months. So . . . almost three. Needless to say, we weren't close.

Kaleb is
26 months
today !!!

Guys who hear "Crazy Train" and sing out "Ay, ay, ay"

I know it's a tic or something like Tourette's where it's literally uncontrollable, but that doesn't make it less annoying. For as long as I can remember, when Ozzy's guitars start rocking that song, dudes bust out the opening no matter where they are. It's seriously like they can't help themselves. I was once in a bar where it played on the jukebox and fifty of them sang it out. Painful!

• • •

People who bite their nails all the way to the white half moon thing

I'm sorry but ew. I was a nail biter as a child and it drove my parents crazy, but my nibbling was more of the grooming variety rather than mutilation. I basically bit off the long white part; but sometimes on other people I see it go down all the way to the nub like Frodo's and it freaks me out.

Juice cleanse people

You want your green juice? Go for it! Enjoy! But why oh why can't people do it in secret? You know, you don't have to tell everyone you know how great you feel, right? It's kind of like the lady doth protest too much: "I feel *so great* and have *sooo much energy!*" Sure ya do. Naturally you don't hear about the hunger pangs and diarrhea.

Burning Man evangelists

Make it stop. Please. My friend Trip, whom I adore more than anything and who is Sadie's beloved godfather, brought a guy to dinner at my house once. The guy seemed affable enough during cocktails, but somehow when we sat down to eat, someone mentioned the word *desert*, which sent him on a thirty-minute solo rant, pontificating on the myriad benefits of the annual festival. I heard about the bartering and the camaraderie in the sand, and the pieces of papyrus everyone wrote their sins or bad memories on and how they put them all in a Smurf village house and set it on fire. Just sitting through his diatribe was hell-ish enough—I know physically going would be an actual trip to Hades.

Mimes

Don't even get me started on those fuckers. As one of the most talkative humans alive, I can't imagine there isn't some darkness underneath the white-painted face and creepy black tears. Stay away. When Dustin Hoffman pushed one to the ground in *Tootsie*, I felt less alone in the world.

Guys with ZZ Top beards who are not in ZZ Top

Dude, I know you're an artisanal pickle maker in Bushwick, but must you have an ISIS-length belly-rubbing beard? It's a trend that is so off-putting, because so many of them would actually be cute if I pinned them down and took a Gillette to that pile of chin pubes.

People who put those crinkly stretch headbands on babies

Sorry, moms, but that shit is akin to child abuse.

•   •   •

Men who ask for their guac mild

Now, this is a personal experiment I have conducted and I can attest: Men who have mild guac suck in bed. Get some fucking spice up in there, lame-o! Maybe they don't want firerrhea and spicy poo burning their anii or something but it's *snoozeville.* Do not go home with a guy who orders that.

People who have Bumper Badgers

Guys, live a little! Yes, your bumpers won't have scratches, that's the good news. The bad news is, you look like a massive idiot with the words *Bumper Badger* emblazoned on your ride. Seriously, that's like people who keep plastic on their furniture or use paper plates at home because they don't want to potentially break china. We're all gonna be dead, so just fucking live and be free. Carpe the fucking diem, yo.

Moms with pigtails

Okay, if you're going to the gym or skiing, great, get that hair back any way you want. But I've seen moms trying to look cool and mellow with low piggies with their overalls or some other trappings of youthful not-giving-a-shitness and it bugs.

Men in mandals

Put those toes away! Flip-flops are one thing, but full elaborate footwear to roam the streets with hairy toes is unacceptable unless you're in the rural Pacific Northwest. I see guys walking around New York all the time in Birkenstocks or Jesus sandals, and while I thought it was so hot in *300*, they were ancient Spartans, not modern cosmopolites.

Chinese restaurant people who swear there is no MSG

Liars! They lie. I always say, "No MSG," which I think somehow translates to "extra MSG." I know this because my fingers swell into kielbasa-size snausages and the only rings that would fit me are Hula-Hoops.

Self-proclaimed oenophiles

Sorry, but I don't care about the tannins. Go see *Sideways* and knock yourself out at some wino circle jerk, but it's so snobby when people take the wine list and say, "Allow me—I'm a real oenophile." If it's red and comes from Château Screwcap or even a fucking box, give me an IV drip and I'll polish that shit off. Your three-hundred-dollar bottle is wasted on me.

Southern women in Manhattan

Okay, now, I have friends living all over the South. I have some southern friends living here in New York, as well. *But* even they will admit there is a particular breed that moves here and is hell-bent on climbing the social ranks. And unlike brash New Yorkers, who wear all their aggression or ambition on their sleeves, these dames all have big smiles and bake for Brick Church or join charity boards but can be the most gossipy backbiting "ladies" you have ever seen! It's all sugary smiles but schadenfreudey news of affairs and whose apartment was twenty mill, or whose kid was rejected by eight schools. Oh, their little blond boys are all in smocked overalls, girls' T-strap shoes, and Little Lord Fauntleroy velvet jackets, but they are, BTdubs, the first ones to punch your kid in the face.

People in the audience at the Oscars who clap harder for some dead people than other dead people

Guys, that's so mean! I know, I loved Robin Williams so much, too, but that old-timey gaffer was a person, too! Heartbreaking.

People who don't clean up their mess of empty sugar packets and spilled skim at Starbucks

Bitch, pick up your shit. It's just rude! I am the custodian of my local Starbucks, cleaning up those soggy straw wrappers and stray stirrers. Fuck, people!

Weaklings who put their fingers in their earholes when an ambulance drives by

I'm sorry but it's just not that loud! Sure, it can be jarring, but buck up, it's not earsplitting, you pussies!

· · ·

♡ ♡

Women who get wet from Michael Bublé's voice

Okay, I heard that there was even one who claimed that she had an orgasm with no other stimulation than the sound of his croon. Now, if I had been present when this woman said this, I would have done an actual eighth-grader bullshit sneeze in her face, but it's simply hearsay. The man who melts hearts and jizzes champagne could never even slightly dampen my Calvins, so I just find it hard to believe. To each her own . . .

PREGNANT WITH A TV SHOW

I swear it was nearly 99 degrees in New York during the last months of my first pregnancy. My swollen feet were the size of the *Intrepid*, with pig-in-a-blanket toes shoved into tragic flip-flops. My skinny single friends were all having sexy, balmy summers, dancing on tables at Sunset Beach on Shelter Island or at Bungalow 8 in New York City. I was a beached whale, sans the crowd of Greenpeace supporters that beached whales usually garner (and sans the beach; I stayed in the city).

Throughout my pregnancy I'd seen the Bugaboo-pushing mommy clique crossing Fifth Avenue in stilettos. They had clearly all "bonded in Lamaze," or preggo yoga or while ordering custom crib linens and bumpers. They chatted about "wheels up" time for NetJets to Aspen and/or how "the traffic is such a bitch to Teterboro." I watched them carefully during my first pregnancy. I found this preened pack interesting, but I couldn't relate.

When I got close to the gaggle on occasion, they freaked me the fuck out. Once, one of them asked when I was scheduling an elective C-section. Uh ... what? Three other knocked-up ladies confronted me in a semicircle when they heard about my barbaric plan to give birth via vag like a coconut-cracking savage. "You absolutely must get a cesarean. It's all planned and you get a blowout and mani and it's just slice 'n' dice!" Like everything else on the Upper East Side, it seemed that giving birth was a matter of "staffing up" and getting the "right" people, process, and look. After all, you want to look fierce in that postsurgery selfie.

"Believe me," said another, leaning in conspiratorially, "your husband will thank you for going C. Mine sure did," with a *my-vagina-is-tighter-than-yours-you-debased-mammal* wink.

Newsflash: Peer pressure works. At my next appointment I asked my gyno about the possibility. She shut the discussion down right away, saying she only did *emergency* C-sections, unlike some of her colleagues, the "society" OBs who would literally cut around a Duke basketball game or a trip to Eden Rock. I shared how some women I knew reacted as if delivering through the birth canal was like standing in a forest and shitting out your baby like a caveperson. My gyno laughed and told me to get used to that kind of attitude. She predicted I'd hear many such judgments for the next twenty years. Of course, she was right. The mommy clique hated the name Sadie and thought it was "too old lady" (I prefer "Ellis Island chic"). Later I would get opinions about how and how long to nurse, how to swaddle, how to baby-proof, how to get my baby walking earlier, how to guarantee a Mozart, an Einstein, the works. Much later there was the mom who told me she thought it was "wildly inappropriate" that I brought my twelve-year-old to the Broadway show *Hedwig and the Angry Inch*, which is about a transgender woman. I told her it was really just about love and being yourself. I got a snort and an eye roll in reply. And once a girl teased Sadie for not having a country house or stables, and her mother emailed me, furious after Sadie replied, "I don't care, I hate horses anyway."

Early on, I was vulnerable to this shit because I was a first-time preggo. And also because I had the worst case of placenta brain in history. I felt like a complete pointy-capped dunce, so was open to "advice." I was scatterbrained and forgetful. I'd walk into a room and forget what I went in for, like my great-grandma. And I was supersensitive.

And the judgyness didn't stop with pregnancy and childbirth, which, by the way, was in a supply closet filled with latex gloves piled to the ceiling. It was fucking *Ecuador*. My gyno said it was the worst birth boom she'd seen in her career: The halls were filled with screaming, laboring women and there was a two-hour wait for epidurals. I wanted to write an article called "Don't Have a Baby in July," because the new moron residents turn over and blindly prick you seven times before finding a vein, but also it's jam-packed, 'cause when it starts to get colder in November, everybody bangs. Hence summer baby boom.

I eventually got morphine and was judged for that, which would only be the beginning. Little did I know, I would be a walking, talking target for unsolicited advice from strangers in cafés about my kid not having enough layers, having too many layers, how to hold her, that she shouldn't be eating that, etc.

When Sadie began walking, I signed up for a baby activity class, not knowing a soul. When I first wheeled in with my shitty stroller, I felt like it was middle school all over again, with people looking each other over and, worse, looking each other's kids over. I smiled and was friendly but felt oddly shy, even though I'm the least shy person on the planet. But I didn't have a wingman and clearly didn't have all the proper gear or lingo or locavore green-eco-sustainable-organic baby snacks.

The teacher came in and sat down cross-legged and asked everyone to sit in a circle. Sadie was running around and I patted the floor next to me and said, "Sadie, sweetie, can you come sit down Indian-style?"

Vinyl record scratch. It wasn't even crickets, it was gasps.

My eyes met those of two *horrified*-looking ladies, who were whispering and looking at me. "What?" I asked, nervous.

"Um, no, it's fine, I mean, it's just—no one says Indian-style anymore. You're supposed to say crisscross applesauce."

Oh.

This sounds melodramatic, but because of: (a) extreme sleep deprivation, and (b) the *Godfather* day of my period which made my bedsheet look like a *Law & Order* crime scene with police tape around the four posts, I was fighting back tears. I smiled and did the class with a lump in my throat, but inside I wanted to scream and cry. *Fucking crisscross applesauce! Are you fucking kidding me?!* I hated these people. They all dressed the same: white skinny jeans and Tory Burch flats. They all bought the same gourmonster ten-dollars-a-serving baby food and they all had the same boring conversations about The Help (their staff, not the book). *I loathed these moms.* I was an outcast. What to do?

Well, the answer was: Write about it. My husband encouraged me to jot down the ridick encounters I regaled him with, and it helped and was fun. I started thinking about writing a novel about my situation and kept notes on the shit I was seeing daily. All those notes became *Momzillas*, a novel about a loner mom, Hannah, in New York City. Hannah was originally from a red state but was me through and through. The book wound up being published in fourteen languages and NBC bought the adaptation rights. I was euphoric—I imagined a future in which I could comfort women all over who also felt the same way.

Of course, Ivy and Fletch followed Sadie and I continued taking notes—because the lambasting didn't stop. I hated breast-feeding. I nursed Sadie and it killed, complete with bleeding nips, so I threw in the burp cloth after I almost burned down the house sterilizing the Frankenstein pump in a boiled-down pot of water. All three kids are fine, by the way. But you'd think I'd killed an endangered animal the way the mommy clique judged me.

"How is the nursing coming?" one momzilla asked.

"Oh, I'm bottle-feeding, actually," I said.

She looked at me the way a ninety-three-year-old looks at an ATM.

Her response: "Shame on you."

Normally I would have a million retorts from "It's really none of your goddamn business" to "Stop about the immunities, it's not like I'm living in the fucking Congo!" but instead I muttered something about different strokes, turned the corner to Seventy-fourth Street, and *burst* into tears. There's something so weirdo and entitled about people who just barrel-ass in with their two cents—I wanted to build a fortress around my family out of all the piles of copper pennies people chucked my way and shield them from the white noise of every idiot, staffed-up socialite who considered herself an expert in parenting my children.

Years passed and I still hadn't really found my mom posse. Five to seven P.M. with little kids and no close friends makes a girl lonely. And makes her drink. I know this sounds alcoholicky, but I couldn't've gotten through those early years without my vino. I cracked the Pinot Noir at 4:59 on many an occasion. I rarely poured a second glass, but I practically shook as I removed the cork until I could guzzle that first one. These days, I have friends who are always up for a tots 'n' tonic—kiddie dinner for the small fries and Bellinis for us—but I didn't have that kind of company in the lonely diaper days when I craved that company the most.

Momzillas, the show, never got made, and I realized from watching network television that even if it had, it never would've had the chutzpah and soul I'd've wanted. I wrote more novels and then eventually wound up writing an essay collection to try to give voice to some of those same issues. It was called *Sometimes I Feel Like a Nut* and it really crystallized what would become the voice of the TV show I wanted to make one day.

When I met with the fabulous Andy Cohen and my personal goddess Lara Spotts at Bravo, we were exploring television ideas, because they thought I could be a good fit for one of their reality shows. I was flattered but made it clear that I could never tolerate a camera up my sphincter or peeking into my marriage and kids' lives—I wanted to write! I pitched a morning show called *Wake the Fuck Up*, which was essentially a late-night-show format but on in the morning, when moms were awake to watch it. They politely passed, as they don't have morning programming like that, but wanted to keep discussing how we could work together.

I sent them both *Momzillas* and *Nut* and asked if, gee, since NBC and Bravo are part of the same conglomerate family, couldn't they just kinda reach over and take my book back and make that? I've since learned a lot about corporate red tape and, alas, it just doesn't work like that. Over time and a really collaborative development process, we made the pilot for what is now the show I love to work on.

My hope for *Odd Mom Out* was and is to make people—not just moms!—guffaw by holding up a mirror to one contingent of the mom population, the epicenter for extreme parenting, where toddlers learn Mandarin 'cause their Goldman Sachs daddies say it's "the wave of the future" and people hire different consultants for walking, talking, peeing, pooing, and proper pencil grip. Most people in America are keeping up with the Joneses, but New Yorkers are keeping up with the Rockefellers. And we can't! Because even wealthy people here can feel middle class compared with those whose wealth was created by recent economic booms. Recently I saw north of twenty Escalades outside a school near me—with a drop-off and pickup fashion show worthy of a catwalk. Yes, I dress up compared to most people in America every day because I wear skirts or dresses and heels instead of pants and sneakers. (But, in fairness, stilettos feel like sneakers to me, like those Easy Spirit commercials with nuns playing basketball.) Nevertheless, at the preschool in my all-black Club Monaco and Trash and Vaudeville motorcycle jacket, I often felt like everyone else was so perfectly preened and polished and that the dismissal catwalk was sponsored by Mercedes-Benz.

My daughter Ivy once asked me, "Mom, why are you the only mom at school without red bottoms on your shoes?" I didn't know whether to be proud she was observant or horrified that she somehow gleaned Louboutin's status by osmosis. But whether it's winning hockey tournaments or making the cheerleading squad—the yardstick from state to state may shift—the stress of fierce competition seems universal. When *Momzillas* came out, I was amazed how many letters I got from midwestern, southern, and Pacific northwestern states, saying that despite the change of metropolitan scenery and shifting metric of aspiration, it was the same exact thing. Mothers-in-law from hell are the rule and not the exception, social climbers abound, and money talks. *Odd Mom Out* seems to have hit a similar nerve. I like to think that it'll help people see outside the judgmental forces and flush them out of their consciousness, grab the kiddies, blare some *Hedwig*, and dance on top of all those unsolicited opinions.

♡ ♡

YOU'RE THE ONE
THAT I WANT

"A hickey from Kenickie is like a Hallmark card." I didn't quite know what that meant when I first saw *Grease* as a child. I think of Hallmark cards as lame and cheesy, but subsequently learned that in the 1950s they were considered *really* special. And the famed greaser sidekick adds, "When you care enough to send the

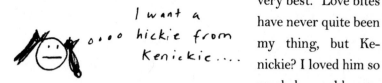

I want a
o·o·o hickie from
Kenickie....

very best." Love bites have never quite been my thing, but Kenickie? I loved him so much he could vampire me to death. But for the adoring lash-batting masses, it was Kenickie's best friend, Danny Zuko, the star, who seemed to be the one every girl swooned over.

But I have never been every girl.

When everyone loved Ferris, I fell for tragic Cameron. When hordes screamed for the throaty front man at the rock concert, I oogled the hot bassist. Again and again, my "type" is that I have no type, other than that he is always the one overshadowed by his glowier friend, the supernova who makes the other girls faint. But not me. Fuck the starlight—it's the night sky that makes them pop anyhow. The darker sidelined characters always revved my engine louder.

When *Grease* hit theaters around the world, its prized headliner was sealed in as a heartthrob. My father called him "John Revolting." While other girls wrung their Calvins over Zuko, I chundered at the thought—he was Puko to me. Even when it was nostalgia cool to dig him during his *Pulp Fiction* renaissance when the brilliant Tarantino fished him out of the career shitter and christened him Vincent Vega avec royale with cheese, I loved the familiarity and kitsch value but could've hurled at the thought of fucking him. I mean, ew.

Not because of his Scientology or his lupine features, but because of the ghost of Zuko past. This is a guy who was such a pussified assface that he ditched Sandy (who played serious tonsil hockey with him in the waves that summer), when his pals ridiculed her enthusiastic greeting. He had to say, "That's my name, don't wear it out!" prompting shrill Aussie shrieks of "You're not the Danny Zuko I met at the beach!" Yeah, well, fuck him. And that Goody-Two-shoes with her dumb chucked pom-poms? She was sweet but they both sucked, if you asked me. And what a lame lesson their so-called "love" proved: Change yourself completely and then the other person will like you!

I myself have always been more of a Rizzo-type of girl. In fact, I played her in my high school musical senior year. Screw blond, pretty, and perfect; I much more identified with the tough cookie. Not that I was banging in backseats or planning to Dyson out a fetus if I ever got knocked up, but that somehow seemed edgier than some cheerleading blonde with *Dumb and Dumber* bangs.

And why did I feel this way? Because the knocker-upper, the bad boy with the heart of gold, the stud who put the sizzling grease in "Greased Lightning," was my very first heartthrob. Kenickie.

It's still unclear what kind of a fucking name that is. I've yet to hear of another before or since. But that guy slayed me. They sang "The chicks'll cream" and, while I was too young to "cream" (vom, BTdubs), I do remember, as a small child of six or seven, being turned on by him. I know! Paging Dr. Freud. I look at my young daughters and swear they don't get aroused by movie stars, but who the fuck knows. It's not like I broadcasted it. I think my mom just thought I really dug the music.

I opened my vinyl double album cover and would stare at him for hours. I watched the movie on our spanking-new VHS player and wore that tape into the ground. So smitten was I by Kenickie, I used to tiptoe into my parents' living room in the dark (which was a big deal for me) to borrow/steal an antique magnifying glass my father had bought. It had an ivory handle and rested on a mahogany table. The poor dead elephant tusk, warped crystal, and I would pore over the group photos of faux-yearbook collages and find Kenickie. Sigh . . . He was beautiful. He was flawed. He was everything. *Pourquoi?*

Some answers: First of all, he was drawn to the strong woman. He didn't care that Riz was a bit of a ballbuster. She made pronouncements, spoke her mind, and wasn't afraid to ruffle feathers. In order to protect herself, she played it cool when she thought she had a bun in the oven. When "good news traveled fast" at the drive-in, Kenickie says he doesn't run away from his mistakes, lending instant support and a hand on her shoulder. Jeff Conaway, the actor who played my beloved, looked positively crushed when Stockard Channing coolly replied, "It's someone else's mistake." You can almost see the hurt conjuring up a mist of tears in his eyes as he looks away and says, "Thanks a lot, kid." The chink in his leather armor melted me.

For her own emotional shield, Rizzo takes up with Kenickie's pockmarked white-trashtastic rival, who somehow has procured a vehicle with actual flames shooting out of its tailpipes. Humiliated, Kenickie sadly follows suit by escorting the at-least-twenty-nine-year-old Cha Cha DiGregorio to their high school prom. But it's all an empty gesture meant to balance the scales of infidelity—Kenickie watches, forlorn, as crater cheeks holds his sassy vixen in red. Social-climbing and whorish Cha Cha ditches him anyway, scoring the dance prize with Zuko, who once again eclipses his hotter, cooler, sexier pal.

When Riz finally sheds her uterine lining and has a most welcome flag of Japan in her panties, she runs back into Kenickie's arms, elatedly declaring a false alarm. They embrace beneath the Ferris wheel mid-carnival.

In my opinion, it is the kiss of the movie. Fuck the leather pants and cigarette-smoking poseur of Sandy or newly christened jock Zuko in his varsity letterman sweater—they each changed who they were to land the other, like a sick, twisted version of "The Gift of the Magi," where it wasn't about generosity but assimilation and subversion of identity. Lame. Kenickie loved Rizzo in all her adventurous, shimmy-down-the-drainpipe glory! That cunt Patty Simcox may have gossiped about his girl, but Kenickie didn't give a shit about those preened, ponytailed, student council sock-hop boppers. Sandy had to get a total makeover from that train wreck Frenchy to land her man. Rizzo was just herself.

But back to her paramour, Kenix.

My best friend Vanessa's fabulous late mother, Nancy, memorably advised us one night on her Martha's Vineyard porch: "Like the guys who like you." She didn't understand the concept of chasing down some playboy, some project to work on, a man to morph. *Like the guys who like you.* Perhaps because I identified with Riz long before I played her, I liked the one who selected her—not because she put out, but because she was fierce. She was all woman. Opinionated, silly, sexy, badass. How hot is it to find a guy who's drawn to that rather than poodle skirts? I'm not ragging on Sandy because she never had a drink or pierced ears or had a dick in her; I think she sucked because she's a one-way ticket to snoozeville! Riz was never boring—she was the life of the slumber party, after all. And Kenickie saw that sparkle and it electrified him. It made him nervous and it made him feel things. Not just in his denim. He was exuberant when smitten, decimated when heartbroken. Lower lows but higher highs. He was in touch with his emotions, which was wildly sexy. I wanted someone just like him—that alluring mélange of a velvet fist in an iron glove. The most intoxicating combination.

Now, granted, his gum chewing and prom outfit left a lot to be desired, but in the purity of his default uniform—jeans, a T-shirt, a necklace that I found scaldingly hot—and his T-Bird leather motorcycle jacket, he made me weak. Every viewing through the decades.

I can honestly say the guy still drives me crazy. Tastes shift, one's own romantic history colors idols or taints types, but Kenickie could've still given me a hickey anytime. In 2011, when I heard Jeff Conaway had died, I was sad the way anyone is when a beloved actor is lost to the world. But what I also buried was a piece of my childhood; I bade adieu not only to my first crush but also to my huge-hearted boy-crazy youth. We jaded adults don't get starry-eyed the way young people do. He was the closest thing to matinee idol for me, but what he did was serve as the first spotlight on my affection for the guy in the wings. The beginning of a personal trend not to seek the star. Not the center of attention but the "lieutenant" (as he happens to call Danny, who takes over for him at Thunder Road and saves the day when Kenickie suffers unfortunate head trauma).

Maybe it's because I knew I could never get the "main guy," so I was drawn to the sidekick, but I think the pack often defines the leader; Danny wanted to impress Kenickie when fawning over Sandy. Steely Riz choked back tears for him. And in the end, it was their smooch that made my heart skip a beat. As for me, I've never gone for the leading stud in my own life. Only the quirky one stage left. We go together like rama-lama-lama-kadingi-da-ding-de-dong. Because those guys always have so much more lightning inside them.

Special Guest chapter!
THE VON BLOG

The Von Blog, by Brooke Von Weber

Dearest readers: We interrupt this essay collection to offer a special guest entry from Brooke Von Weber. People think native New Yorker Jill Weber knows so much about city life, but it turns out Brooke knows waaaaay *more* about everything, so I asked her to excerpt some of her Von Blog, which . . . oddly has a cult following. Enjoy!

Hi, Ladies! Brooke Von Weber, here!

ALL my friends are *constantly* asking me where I bought certain wait-listed accessories, how I get to the Hamptons, et cetera. When everyone's asking you to send them contacts or vendors, it can get a little overwhelming. I figured it was time to consolidate my findings and do the right thing: share. *So*, I hereby present my gift to you: Welcome to Von Blog, my own version of Gloop. I'll be blogging twice a week on "a few of my favorite things," like another Von Mom—Maria von Trapp! But screw whiskers and kettles and strudel. (Who would eat that, anyway?!) My list of must-haves is chic, modern, and has everything an uptown girl would need.

UBER CHOPPER!

Bumper-to-bumper traffic on the LIE making you want to dice up your Prozac and snort it? Me, too. It's just unacceptable that it can take five hours to get to the Hamptons! My sister-in-law, Jill, calls it the Cramptons, which really annoys me, but when I'm staring at the legions of Escalades clogging Montauk Highway, I must admit, I get it! So what to do to avoid the hideous waits? Since my husband, Lex, sold his company (which brought bagels to China, which was just the innovation they needed), it is to the Thirty-fourth Street heliport we go! Rather than torturously sitting in a frazzled state of anxiety, we blithely take off when I say so, via Uber Chopper. Cruising through the air above the East River, we glide over everyone, and get to our destination in thirty-five easy-breezy minutes. You can see the city skyline, and then the Gatsby-style mansions in Locust Valley, where Lex plays golf, followed by farmland and greenery, which is just fabulous for Shipley, McCallister, Rutherford, and Langley and their little city lungs! Not to mention the highway where everyone else is sweating it with brats screaming in the backseat with the help! Thank goodness those days are over. Now we just have the freedom to do what we want, when we want. Bliss! So forget the silly tollbooths and honking headaches—let that propeller propel you where you want to go, faster. Because life is short! Time is money, so let's pay a little to get some back— you'll thank me for it!

·   ·   ·

MERCEDES SPRINTER

I manage so much! Shipley, McCallister, and Rutherford have horrific pickup schedules. It's like Tetris for me trying to organize each of their nannies to be where they need to be. But a whiteboard in the kitchen? An app on my phone? No, thanks. We took our family office mobile with our new Mercedes Sprinter. Sure, it might sound crazy, buying a huge truck used to transport twenty businessmen from conventions to the hotels, or a New Jersey bachelorette party to the Meatpacking District, but we made it all our own. We bought our black Sprinter, had all the insides ripped out, and had it custom retrofitted (or "pimped," if you will) with leather couches around the perimeter, flat-screen televisions, a refrigerator for snacks on the go, handmade cushions and back bolsters, an ottoman, and a trading desk for Daddy. It's heaven on wheels! Why load into a hideous minivan like those people with the curly-hair sideburn things in Brooklyn? The Mercedes Sprinter may seem enormous for a personal vehicle, but if you think of it as an extension of your home, then you'll get it. My decorator, Bradley, worked with the gentlemen at the design firm that also created the interiors of our jet, and they did such a wonderful job. From the trims on the drapes to the wonderful carpet lining the floor, our drop-off process feels like a rolling living room!

GLAMSQUAD

Isn't it such a drag to haul ass to some salon, only to run into all your friends there pre-hairwash? And, really, do I want that pushy class mom to see me in a towel turban? *Hell* to the no! That's why I use Glamsquad. It's an app on your iPhone and it's basically the Uber of hair and makeup. Minus the rapes. Cool stylists and artists come over and blow out your locks before a function and beat down your face till you're red carpet ready. Whenever they come over, I feel like a million bucks afterward! If I wanted a *Steel Magnolias* moment, I'd call my annoying sisters. But I don't. I can even get my nails done at the same time! Last time, I had a pedicure technician, hair sculptor, and lash specialist all at the same time! I felt like Cleopatra. Luckily without the asp! So next time you gotta get glam, use the squad. Anything else is just an extra errand. Happy flashbulbs!

CRONUT

Okay, so perhaps you wouldn't actually consume this thousand-calorie confection—it's the world-famous combo of a croissant and doughnut in a blender (or cookie sheet) but do you really want to say you've never even tasted one? Provincial tourists and Japanese guidebook toters have all sampled their buttery goodness, so why not you? The wait, of course. Endless! The average is an hour and a half, and as a mother of four, I simply haven't got that kind of time. But you can pay people to do it for you! There is a whole cottage industry springing up of people who are desperate for dough! So for McCallister's class party, I hired ten people to wait in line, since the maximum purchase is two Cronuts. And voilà! I got my precious pastries. They cost hundreds of dollars, but you can't buy PR like people buzzing that you served Dominique Ansel pastries at a first-grader's party, am I right? It's nice to teach kids to appreciate the little luxuries. Anyone can have a cake, but I say, let them eat Cronuts!

A CHIC NAME

Can't get into the new It cantina? Try adding a *von* to your name! Well, we didn't add the von, of course. As my mother-in-law, Candace, said, we restored it. *If a Cézanne were chipped, you would restore it, yes?* Well, so goes a name. As it turns out, you can hire a genealogist to excavate the roots of your family tree, even if the trail gets fuzzy after your dead grandparents. If they don't find anything, you can always buy a title! Seriously. There are nobles who squandered their fortunes through the generations and are now dirt poor. So they sell their *de* or *van* or *di* or *della*, and it can be all yours. There are just so many counts without accounts. So plunder their crest and start a new chapter! It opens doors and checkbooks. My fundraising tripled when I solicited money for my NACHO gala. People want aristocratic names on their boards and all charity is tit for tat. I'm happy to take my place in society as a philanthropist, and it helps when you have the history of an old illustrious family backing you.

WHEELS UP

Do you really want to go through one of those toxic X-ray machines at the airport? Be herded with immigrants from god knows where, wearing god knows what? I sure don't. That's why Lex and I charter exclusively. If it's pricey, just split it with your friends! It's a worthy investment—just think about the protection to your health. There's so much less of a risk of contracting Ebola or hepatitis F. You don't want to hear incessant coughs where chunks of lung are propelled through the cabin. Even in first class, Lex and I had a passenger behind us who was spraying sneezes into the air nonstop! I say: Life's too short. It's time to fire up the bird and depart when you want, not when Charlie Brown's teacher announces it.

A BABY NURSE (FOR A YEAR)

Moms, listen up. I've heard it all: Baby nurses are a racket, it's three hundred dollars per day, etc. But let me tell you something:

It's an investment in your beauty sleep. It's hard enough having a newborn and recovering from your elective C-section. But if you have the proper nurse on hand, she can worry about sleep training while you heal! It's a no-brainer, really. Be sure when you interview nurses to avoid ones on the hefty side. One mother I knew woke up at 10 A.M. and went into the nursery to find her newborn screaming in his crib with the baby nurse dead on the floor from a heart attack! Her little ticker had stopped tocking and couldn't support her load. So my friend had to start interviewing new nurses and was alone with her baby! So I say, trust trim. If they can't control their waistlines, how can they control your child?

KIBU THE JAPANESE DOG WALKER

If you're a dog lover like I am, you need Kibu. And by dog lover, I do not mean adopting some mutt at the shelter. We were on the wait-list for seven years for a Cavalier King Charles spaniel from those famous lesbian breeders in Minnesota, and, let me tell you, it was worth every second. Farnsworth is a delight (it's a family name), and I wouldn't trust anyone to care for him other than Kibu. The famed dog walker of the Upper East Side may look interesting with his long straight hair reaching his backside, and his head-to-toe Rick Owens postapocalyptic leather outfits are a bit on the eccentric side, and he may charge two hundred dollars per day per dog, but he's a gem. You have to be on your best behavior when he comes over to interview you. Offer him drinks and chef-made hot hors d'oeuvres (he loves caviar) and he will interrogate you—I mean, question you—about your dog. *If* he accepts you, you've hit the dog owner lottery—you must thank him with a gift. He loves Vuitton or Goyard messenger satchels! He will then commence duties with your dog's doodies! I can be so clever sometimes! Each week, he will give you a laminated Microsoft Excel spreadsheet with a complete fecal and behavior report, which we keep in a T. Anthony binder in the front hall. If I were dyslexic, I'd say "I thank dog for Kibu!" There I go again, being funny!

J. MENDEL SAMPLE SALE

Role up your cashmere sleeves and "get ready to rumble"! It's the annual J. Mendel sample sale! The forty-thousand-dollar coats are only twenty-two thousand, and all of the city is in a *frenzy*. It's a mad fit of bargains galore and shoppers' high. When you arrive, there will be many aggressive Horace Mann moms ready to claw their way to your sable. So here's what I do. Slip someone at the Madison boutique a grand or two. Have them give you the floor plan of the garment district showroom where they have the sales. Then, when you walk in, you can bolt for the sheared minks or whatever you desperately need! It's pandemonium and only a savvy shopper will score the key deals. You need to act fast and pounce or you'll miss out, and you'll lie awake traumatized that some beeyotch drove home with your chinchilla. Preparation yields prizes.

FASHION WEAK

I've long had a penchant for making cartoon doodles (as you can see in this book!). I've been at it since my ammo was a number two pencil and my canvas the margins of my calculus notebook. My work is a little more sophisticated (content-wise, anyway) now—G-rated swirly initials of my crush du jour inside stylized hearts have given way to my own line of greeting cards through a letterpress printer in Brooklyn (Coeur Noir, available on Etsy, yo!). One of my favorites is a tiny smiley face on the front of the card and then inside it says:

A LITTLE HEAD FOR YOUR BIRTHDAY.

A couple of years ago I got a call from a woman who had seen some of my doodles—maybe she'd seen the cards, or maybe she'd seen some of the ones that made it into *Sometimes I Feel Like a Nut*. But she was a fan and asked if I wanted a fun gig: Would I like to decorate the café inside the tents at New York's Mercedes-

Benz Fashion Week. *Moi?!* I was elated, of course. But I asked if she understood I was sort of "out there" and, well, irreverent. Yup, she got that. I asked if I could do some funny tongue-in-cheek fashion commentaries. Totes magotes. I asked if I needed to show sketches first or just let 'er rip.

"Let 'er rip, just do whatever you want," she replied. "I'm running the whole thing, so you can seriously do anything—just do you!"

Has another artiste ever heard such ego-stroking words?! *So thrilling!*

She went on to explain that there would be a large room within the cavernous pavilion for the café and it would be painted with black chalkboard paint. I would have free rein to decorate it with my chalked handwriting and doodles, banners, and comic strips. And, she said, an assistant would email me to arrange for whatever supplies I needed, as well as with instructions about where to show up and when.

Heaven!

For days leading up to the event, I was walking on air; suddenly I was—technically—a working artist! I would be paid to draw—how cool is *that?* The day arrived—two days before the fashion shows would be put on—and it was a blustery and cold winter day. The short walk to the location froze my face and made it an uncharacteristic dark and chapped red. At least, I thought, the tent would be heated and I'd thaw out while working. I was mistaken.

I was greeted cheerily by my contact but also dozens of construction workers, one of whom handed me a yellow hard hat. Two days to go and they were still building this shit hole? It was a glacial war zone I'd be working in. They gave me ladders and a scaffold, which made me feel kind of Michelangelo-y, but I could see my breath; the Arctic temps canceled my Renaissance church-decorating fantasies pretty quickly. Nonetheless I got to work. I selected a pristine piece of yellow chalk and started to create the café sign. Pretty straightforward.

Then came the menu, which I handled beautifully, I must say. I created killer ribboned banners containing the main subjects, like soups, salads, and sandwiches, which I shortened to "sammies." Cute, right?

Then I got down to the funny business. Next to the menu item "Bagel, $3" I drew an arrow pointing to a large four-by-three-foot comic strip of two fashionistas talking. The cartoon bubble above the stilettoed swans said, "OMMFG you got a BAGEL?! You may as well tape each half to your ass cheeks 'cause that's where it's going!"

A cartoon from the beverages category showed two manorexic guys with shades, one of whom was saying "I'll just have a hot

water with lemon—I'm trying to get down to my birth weight." The other guy said "I need a coffee; I'm so tired from lying awake all night trying to decide if Jack or Lazaro was hotter."

And with a huge arrow I created beautiful signage that read "Ladies' Room to Barf It All Up Two Doors Down on the Left!"

My masterpiece was a border I created to go around the entire café space. Above caricatured audience characters, I created a CNN-like crawl of newsflashy narration in Day-Glo pink chalk: "Front row fashionistas: hot fotogs ... editrixes with sunglasses . . . gasians . . . Tokyo teens . . . bloggers with braces . . . pouting Olsens . . . Botoxed buyers . . . runway roadies . . . red state models . . ." and so on all around the room.

I put down my last piece of chalk at about 6 P.M., after ten hours of straight drawing. My only break had been for a soggy tuna sandwich brought to me midday. My hands were beet red, my bones ice cold. But I was satisfied. I had created something awesome and funny, and I did it all by myself. I was so proud.

I folded up my ladder and leaned it against a side I beam, and went to gather my things. Out of the corner of my eye, I saw a posse that looked straight out of the Sprockets *SNL* skit—in all black with skinny jeans, boots, turtlenecks, and frowns. Assistants with iPads, walkie-talkies, and headsets followed, and their chatter—a rabble-rabble like Charlie Brown's teacher—had a stressy overtone. This mini-mob of clones was coming my way. They were scrutinizing my work. My forehead started to feel hot and my breathing quickened. I had a bad pit of bile blooming in my stomach. Then, my paranoia was confirmed: *"Who is this Jill person? Where is she now?"*

I rose from where I'd been packing my bag on the dusty floor and walked over with my hard hat, introducing myself.

"Uh, hi, I'm Jill Kargman, the cartoonist."

"Yeah, hi," said the guy, who was so thin Karen Carpenter herself would have risen from her grave, looked at him jealously, and then lain back down. "These just will not do."

ME: Will not *do*? Like, what do you mean?

ASSHOLE: I *mean* they're mocking our world. The fashion world.

ME: That's the point. To be funny.

ASSHOLE: Okay, this is just not what I pictured. This is not funny.

ME: Well, I'm so sorry—I was told I would have free rein and be able to do exactly what I wanted creatively.

ASSHOLE: Yeah, no. Sorry, but this all needs to be erased and redone.

ME: Yeah, no.

ASSHOLE: Excuse me?

ME: I was asked by someone in your organization to do this any way I wanted to, and I have spent ten hours in the freezing cold making it, out in the open. No one did anything all day except giggle and tell me how great it was.

ASSHOLE: Well, that's just too bad. It's coming down and I want you to redo it.

ME: Sorry, but if you want it redone you'll have to get someone else.

I handed him my hard hat and walked off, *furious*. In fact, I don't know that I have ever been so annoyed—I wanted to bash his fucking razor-blade-cheekboned face in. *Who* can't laugh about fashion? Even fashion people laugh about fashion!

I left in a rage, livid that the woman who asked me to do it clearly didn't wield as much power as she thought she did (and, BTW, she was nowhere in sight!). Ripshit, I stormed into a nearby bar, bought a glass of wine, and downed it in under a minute, cursing the haughty prick who was ordering my work to be erased as I asked for my second glass.

A week later, I was invited to one of the fashion shows, the Milly collection. No more construction zone. The place sparkled lights and fabrics—no one would have ever known it had looked like Tikrit only days before.

On my way out, I decided to peek at the café. It had been redone with boring, bare-bones lettering and no cartoons anywhere, just plain black walls and utilitarian signage. Yawn. I fantasized how much cooler it would've been to have my killer doodle murals and have people talking about them, but instead it was a snoozeville food stand.

But I learned a lesson: Never lift a fucking finger without a contract. Also: Screw that asshole. Humor makes everything more fun! If his life really is fashion to such an extreme that he can't even laugh at it, he's just a petty power tripper with no life—no matter what his Instagram portrays. 'Cause soon enough that entire mammoth structure came down and his week of reigning supreme was over; he was alone with only models to name-drop and last night's parties to recap. Woo-hoo.

THINGS THAT BEFUDDLE NEW YORKERS

I ♥ NY

The velvet rope line outside Abercrombie & Fitch

Trying to think of a nice way to say this . . . hmmm . . . *What the fuck is wrong with you people?!* You're seriously shvitzing your balls off to get into a lame store?! I mean, that line—rain, sleet, snow, or blazing sun—is ever growing. Every time I walk by, I scratch my head. Even if Dolce & Gabbana were having an 80-percent-off sale, I wouldn't wait in a nightclub line like that to shop. But A&F isn't Dolce, peeps. Its mainstay is tees emblazoned with their logo! They should pay *you* to wear that! Jeez.

People who say Ralph L'Ren

Guys, it's *Lauren.* The accent is on the first syllable. It's not like L'Wren Scott (may she rest). Also annoying is yentas saying Donna K'ran. Especially because ironically these are old Jewesses pronouncing it like the Islamic Bible. It's *Karan*, pronounced just like *Karen*. Like Karen Allen of *Indiana Jones* fame.

Tourists who wait for the Walk sign

Guys, New Yorkers don't see those blinking hands as commands, we see them as *suggestions*. Just jaywalk or use your old-fashioned eyeballs to see if a truck is careening toward you. But if you are going to be a goody-goody and wait-wait through the entire flashing Don't Walk sequence, please step aside, 'cause dis beeyotch got places to be.

People posing with Times Square Elmo

Guys, that's not really Elmo, you know. Inside the not–*Sesame Street*–approved costume (probably made by twelve-year-olds in China), there's a very sweaty person. But go ahead, pay him five bucks for a shot. If you want a real thrill, stick around till three and watch as he pops the head right off and staggers to the subway, red fur from the neck down. The real deal.

Chick-fil-A

What is this poultry chain of which you speak? Alls I know is it hails from some rectangle in the middle and reeks of red state "values," like speaking out against gay people. Nice. So you fry chicken eyelids in a bucket and fatten 'Murica and that's "real" America? Makes so much sense.

How crickets can somehow be louder than sirens

I can blissfully float into slumber mode with a legit fleet of ambulances charging by. But when I visit the country, the cacophony of those slutty crickets doing their mating call drives me off the rails like a crazy train. They are deafening. Give me the mollifying hum of traffic, the honks of home, any night of the week.

TWERKIN' FOR A BIRKIN

Recently overheard while waiting/eavesdropping outside Sadie's Hebrew school:

"You guys, you have to come with me to this stripper class! It's so fun. *So. Fun!*"

Who could possibly not try to listen in on this conversation more? Not me. I leaned my head toward the four rail-thin keratined moms in cigarette-leg spray-on jeans, high boots, leather jackets, trendy handbags, and bling galore.

"Oh, my friend from Horace went! Her body is amaaazing now! *Sick!*"

"It's the best. I feel so *shtrong*. I gave David a lap dance last night, he went nuts. I'm totally twerkin' for a Birkin."

You can't make this shit up! I sprayed a mouthful of iced coffee on the sidewalk (and my coat), which caused the JAP in chief to turn around and glare at me.

"I'm so sorry but I couldn't help but overhear your convo," I apologized, "and I just have got to hear more about this place."

What followed was an animated explanation of how stripping beats SoulCycle, Barry's Bootcamp, private Pilates, AKT dance class, and walks around the reservoir. The pole class, they vouched breathlessly, sculpted them in a whole new way. They gyrated, shimmied, slid down individual poles in the classroom studio, and most important, they proudly shared, they learned to pelvic-thrust the magic back into their fifteen-year marriages.

What was not to like? *Bingo!* I was in.

Right there, while waiting for Sadie to come out of class, I went online to sign up for stripper class the following week. (Has that line ever been written before? No. No, it has not.) I was sure one or more of the four JAPpy amigas would be there, but I wanted to share the experience with someone I actually knew well. I began trolling for someone I could rope into doing this with me. Most of my closest friends work, and those who don't said they couldn't schlep downtown the day I wanted them to. Feeling kind of desperate for company, I tried some of my new-mom acquaintances at kindergarten pickup a couple of days later. "Hey, any of you ladies want to come with me to a stripper pole dance class?"

Crickets. No, like, Cric . . . kets. Then one mom said, "I'm really surprised you would do that. I mean, it sounds really sad."

I stammered, embarrassed, with some Naomi Wolf–ism about takin' the power back or some such, but felt my cheeks reddening. They thought I was a weirdo, learning to shake it with women who were probably saving up to get implants or training to give Champagne room blow jobs in exchange for Benjamins. I could see it in their eyes: I was trash. I was a prostitute.

Without anyone I knew well, I went anyway.

As customary for all my appointments, I arrived approximately twenty-nine minutes early. I am a chronic early bird and have such panic attacks when I think I'm going to be late. I'd rather be a half hour early than five minutes late. So there I was, with nothing to do but obsess about how I was about to do a stripper class and shop the hanging wares.

The reception area doubled as a little stripper-gear boutique—mesh body suits, nippleless bras, thongs galore. I signed in, filling out the necessary forms on a clipboard à la at a medical office: indemnification, how I learned about them, signatures that I wouldn't sue if I slipped and cracked my melon on the studio floor, dance experience, etc. I walked the clipboard of completed forms up to the desk and sat back down. I eyed the other women waiting for class—they all looked younger than me by a good ten years and like, well, strippers. I spied a couple who maybe were pushing late thirties, but even they were basically tits on sticks. I was ten times more intimidated than when I popped my Soul-Cycle cherry.

An announcement was made for the beginner's class and I filed nervously behind the gathered women into a darkly lit dance studio. Except in addition to dance space and mirrors, there were eight poles planted in the floor. Our teacher sashayed in. Not what I expected at all! Instead of greased jugs the size and pert-ness of grapefruits, she was more Joan from *Mad Men:* zaftig, with a huge bosom. And her name wasn't Sapphire or Brandy but something non-stagey like Carol or Stephanie—I don't even re-member her name, I was so stunned.

After a short introduction about the class and the history of the studio, we were asked to go around the circle and explain why we had signed up for the class. One woman said "to feel sexy again." Fair enough. Another, to be "empowered." Okay. Then a cute but frail blond girl meekly admitted, "I am going through a really, really bad divorce and my therapist said I should get out of my shell by doing activities with women." *Sadness*. I wanted to hug her and bail and get wine together somewhere. I went last: I admitted to good old-fashioned curiosity and said I thought the idea sounded fun and funny at the same time.

Time to get started.

Carol/Stephanie asked us all to find a place on a mat and get comfortable. Wait . . . what? What happened to straddling poles 'n' shit?! I wanted some Jennifer Beals action *stat*! But, no, apparently we needed to start with the basics. Level one was about finding our sensuality, she explained while running her fingertips along the border of the mat, as if it were luscious velvet. She had us glide our fingers over our thighs, then up our torsos, up our arms, down our necks, between our boobs. We did this soft touching of ourselves as she quietly whispered things like, "This is how it begins: If you feel sexy, you are sexy. Sometimes my boyfriend wants to watch the game and I just sit near him and start gently stroking myself with my fingertips and before long, the chips and remote are down and he wants me." Her voice was soothing but not at all a turn-on. She had a voice made for books on tape, not phone sex. And for the life of me all I could picture was some depressing messy one-bedroom in north Chelsea or south of Hell's Kitchen, with shit all over the floor and spilled Tostitos.

But I did as I was told: I kept stroking myself until it was time to progress to stroking while standing and then we added slowwww gyrations and then, eventually, finally, we were told to pair off to share a pole. I made a beeline for Divorced Girl. Turns out, she had some serious fire inside her broken soul. She let it out and her mane swirled with her. She seemed lost in thought. The teacher noticed and gave her some solid encouragement. That lit my personal competitive fire—I am not used to not being the teacher's pet—and I decided I needed to rock it. Unfortunately, I made a weird off-putting screeching sound on the pole and looked like a pony trying to ride a pommel lift. I was all slipping hooves and awkward gripping and sad, fried, keratined head pubes instead of flowing, sexy locks. I could tell this wasn't my game. My performance was an instant boner wilter.

This was especially apparent once Carol/Stephanie took the floor. She invited us to sit on our mats (crisscross applesauce, not Indian-style, of course) and then she demonstrated what we could be working toward should we choose to buy a class package and commit to ascending to level five. And then: she dimmed the lights, turned on some music, and had her way with the pole. Writhing and climbing and sliding and rubbing herself. Just seeing her thrashing and undulating made me totally see how guys got hot for that stuff, and this wasn't even with boobs out—it was a fully clothed exhibition! But I couldn't get it up for this form of exercise. I sheepishly thanked the receptionist and bailed sans purchase, never to return. I'm way more turned on by a yummy boozy dinner downtown or going to a funny play. Maybe I'm lazy, maybe I just am not that into Birkins, but I felt more blah than bada-bing. Harry may not be getting lap dances, but on the bright side, he's saving lotsa dough by my skipping swiping plastic at Hermès for that Birkin bag. Sexy dances aren't sexy unless the dancer is feelin' it, and this tired mom just ain't. Plus, we'd both probably burst out laughing anyway.

COCO'S WORDS OF WISDOM

My gorgeous mother was also a source of constant advice for Willie and me growing up, and her guidance went far beyond the don't-fill-up-on-bread-before-a-meal kind of instruction.

Coco has the biggest heart (she tears up during TV commercials. "Here we go," my dad says lovingly as she dabs at her eyes. "Waterworks.") and is one of the most grateful people on earth. Whereas other people preach stopping to smell the roses, she's got hundreds of snaps on her iPhone of flowers she's stopped to notice! She never got us to pray before dinner or anything, but she never failed to remind us how lucky we were when we were about to chow down like animals at the table. Gotta be honest: I attribute my appreciation of my life to her sort of forcibly shoving gratitude down my throat. I remember saying, "Mom, yes, we get it; we're lucky." Then I went and had kids of my own and realized how with me she still is every step of the way.

Some of her nuggets that I cherish are:

"Slow down! Eat everything like it's caviar, because to someone else it is."

My dad, brother, and I used to Dyson down any plate of food my mom placed in front of us. We'd also scarf down every shred of food at restaurants, prompting my mom to get upset because she was looking forward to lingering over the meal and didn't want it to be over so quickly. Bottom line: We are pigs and she is a true lady. But my mom's comment about slowing down was less about manners and much more about truly appreciating food and the ritual of eating a delicious dinner. She hated when we snorted our way through it like animals and instead wanted us to understand that food should be savored and relished. Even if it's something basic, she wanted us to treat it like a delicacy. Now I teach my kids the same thing—and whether it's an artichoke I spent forty minutes boiling or a dish I expertly reheated, I try to keep my mom's advice going at the table. She is such a genius cook, though, I can see why she was doubly distressed. She spent so much time preparing it so we could snarf like wild boars.

"The opposite of a social heavy is a socialite."

The word *socialite* has always bugged me. There were women who my mom said would "go to the opening of an envelope" just to get their pictures taken. Now, she often had obligations for my dad's job but made dinner herself and would always rather be home in her pajamas with us. I have a clear memory of her standing in a pink and white ball gown, wearing red oven mitts and taking our dinner out of the oven. My friend Richard Sinnott, my boss at *Harper's Bazaar*, used to say, "Your mother is the chicest woman in New York; she could be on every society page if she wanted to be." But she didn't want to be. She never used charities to promote herself socially or went out just to be fabulous. On the contrary, her favorite type of night is a cozy one with family.

"You can wear a total schmatte, but if you have good accessories, people will think it's couture."

This is true and I have proven it with a scientific study of one test subject: me. I swear, I can wear a Club Monaco shift or Urban Outfitters skirt, and with the right shoes or bag, people ask me if it's fucking Chanel. It's insane! It always works. Because of that, I rarely invest in designer things (and never buy retail, anyway— I'm a big sale and Woodbury Commons shopper!) unless I can use them all the time. And I don't care what any of these Best Dressed lists say, my mom is the chicest of them all.

"It's all right to cry."

I'm not sure if Kermit the Frog or someone else in the Muppet family sang a song by that name, but it may as well be my mom's and my harmonized anthem. In a world where you often hear "Keep a stiff upper lip," I grew up feeling like it was totally okay to let it out. Not an Olympic Games can be watched without a tissue box handy—and I'm talking curling, people. My mom wells up at movies, shows, commercials, sporting events, concerts, smiling babies, or even just old people holding hands on the street. And I love it. Because I always knew that her comfort with emotions meant I didn't have to bottle mine up.

"By mourning those we love, we live better."

My mom's mom, Nana Sylvette, died of cancer at forty-seven. My aunt Leslie died at fifty, and my uncle at forty-six. On Yom

Kippur, aside from starving, we also remember the loved ones we miss and my mom always has Kleenex at the ready. Her heart is so big that it bursts not only at the sad things but also the sweetest. One of my favorite poems is about the tragedy of loss but also the comfort of memory, and I always hold my mother's hand when we read it:

We Remember Them
by Sylvan Kamens and Jack Riemer

In the rising of the sun
and in its going down,
we remember them.

In the blowing of the wind
and in the chill of winter,
we remember them.

In the opening of the buds
and in the rebirth of spring,
we remember them.

In the blueness of the skies
and in the warmth of summer,
we remember them.

In the rustling of the leaves
and in the beauty of fall,
we remember them.

In the beginning of the year
and when it ends,
we remember them.

When we are weary
and in need of strength,
we remember them.

When we are lost
and sick at heart,
we remember them.

When we have achievements
that are based on theirs,
we remember them.

When we have joys
we yearn to share,
we remember them.

So long as we live,
they too shall live,
for they are a part of us
as we remember them.

SOMEWHERE UNDER THE RAINBOW

I remember the moment I became a gay rights activist like it was yesterday. I was in wood shop. Yes, you read that correctly, *wood shop*. You see, at my Connecticut boarding school, I learned upon arrival that there was not just varsity and junior varsity but also something called thirds. In other words, the lame-o leftovers. They got to play on a field that was a mile away and had games that started as the sun was setting, after the two more important teams had finished and done their high-five chain/parade thingy. Fuck that. But I wasn't allowed to be in a play every semester as my ex, or exercise. So I took aerobics. But I wasn't allowed to take aerobics twice, either, so the third semester, since I despise sports, I found myself in wood shop with all dudes.

A bunch of athletes were in the off-season of their two sports. A couple were fashioning boxes to stash their marijuana, and I set out to make a chair for my dorm room. But within fifteen minutes or so, the tides turned, when one of the pricks (think James Spader's Steff in *Pretty in Pink*) started talking about someone and calling him a "flaming faggot."

I felt the blood run out of my face.

It was in that singular moment that I became obsessed with speaking up.

"You can't say that word!" I blurted. To seniors. "That's a horrible word. That word comes from when they burned homosexuals on faggots of wood!"

With my righteous, violent rant, I also knew I'd sealed my fate as a semi-weirdo there. I already didn't fit in and clung to my closest friends, Lauren and Lisa, who were more normal and social than I, but the truth was I was lucky because I didn't really give a shit. I think I was born with a faulty Edit button, and when most people grow a huge one in high school, mine just disappeared.

Ashamed, the dudes went back to their pot boxes.

See, they didn't even know gay people or hebes like me—some may have thought I got my horns removed via scalpel before I arrived. I grew up not only in New York City, a land far more diverse than whence these Aryan Nation bros hailed, but also in a family that always had gay friends around and actual gaybors, gay next-door neighbors. The decorator Peter Dunham was my childhood next-door neighbor, and all his amazing friends came by; and as a tween I'd go after school in my plaid pinafore and plop down on his couch. I remember music playing and cooking smells and lots of laughter. Christopher Mason, the well-known New York songwriter and performer, played the piano as I lounged in knee socks. My dad worked at Chanel, so we often met fashion-affiliated editors, writers, and executives; and at our dinner parties I was always drawn to the gay male couples, and remember asking one pair of older antiques dealers if they were married. They laughed and explained that they couldn't get married. I remember now how they giggled, as if to say *She's naïve/sweet, that's funny, as if.*

In college, my best friend, Trip, and I talked and made a pact that if we didn't meet the right guys and were both single at twenty-nine (which felt so old at the time), we would have a baby together. I honestly would have been perfectly happy with that route had I not met the right guy, who, as it turns out, was Harry, a very gay-friendly person who never recoiled with homophobic awkwardness like one person I dated. In fact, Harry was so chill about his own sexuality that we went to a gay watering hole, Marie's Crisis, after dinner on our very first date. I appealed to him to donate to equal rights charities, and when he wanted to start buying art (that would be within reach of young collectors), I brought him to a benefit for marriage equality, where gay artists donated their work to raise money for the legal battle ahead, and he was totally game. I couldn't have asked for a more committed partner in my wish to make gay marriage legal. We definitely got into more than a few debates with people who would say domestic partnership was more or less the same thing. But I was sickened to think anyone deserved anything other than the same rights as breeders.

So after growing up in a world of gay men who truly thought the day would never come, I was over the moon—or, uh, rainbow—when SCOTUS delivered the historic decision. And it just so happened that fifteen years after Harry and I met and began sharing that cause, both of us marched in the gay pride parade together. Years prior, Trip had directed an award-winning off-Broadway play called *The Last Sunday in June* that was about pride weekend, and how some gay men were disgusted by the whole thing and opted out of marching beside grouped gay stereotypes like bears in leather vests over flesh with chauffeurs' hats or transvestites with boas. They didn't want to sweat glitter and shit diamonds, they just wanted to have rights without yelling about it. I remember watching that play and understanding both sides—the activists and the ones on the sidelines, as some people are more strident than others. But change always comes with voices, and I have always been a loudmouth.

So when the PR gurus Sandra Lajoie and Liz Schmidt from Bravo arranged for me to ride on the NBC Universal float with Doogie Howser, I was beside myself with elation. In the end, though, rather than be on a double-decker bus, I wanted to walk in the front among the crowds. Staci Greenbaum, our costume designer for *Odd Mom Out,* made me a white Peter Pan–collared blouse with our show's logo on it and a rainbow bow pinned at the top.

From the first minutes walking down the street festooned with waving rainbow flags and cheers and music, I heard people chanting "We love *Odd Mom Out,*" and I realized we had a huge gay audience. I've been lucky enough to be so supported by the gay community with my books—in fact, at one reading at the now-defunct Borders in Atlanta, I was expecting moms and found a crowd of mostly gay black guys. Needless to say, it was the best stop on my tour. As for the show, I had already suspected we had a gay following from various tweets that cheered me on with things like "werq" and "yas queen," but being immersed in the gay community of viewers—on such an historic day, no less— was absolutely a magical high. After a thirty-block walk, we turned onto Christopher Street and I burst into tears. Granted, I was totally on my flag of Japan, on the Godfather day, no less, but I was beyond emotional. It was so breathtaking to go from the wide vista of Fifth Avenue, across to the legendary, winding West Village street that became a symbol of the gay community after the Stonewall riots of 1969. When we got to the famed bar, people were dangling from the rooftops and every window and step. I saw a gay man with one arm who had a unicorn outfit, who yelled "I love you, unicorn!" and I giggled through my veil of tears. It was truly one of the happiest days and experiences of my entire life. Even the Hassidick Jews (I spelled that wrong on purpose) screaming they would all burn didn't get me down. We were on the right side of history and they looked Stone Age at the Stonewall.

We went to the Pier Dance afterward and shimmied with people in rainbow angel wings, platform glitter heels, leather chauffeurs' hats, and vests over chests. Or barely anything at all. During a dance of thousands of people (mostly guys—apparently the lesbz were the day before), I danced smack into my friend Marcello who was newly engaged and with his husband-to-be. They both rocked eight-pack abs (not six—eight) and some sort of banana hammock situation. We hugged and I told him it was one of the best days of my life. I couldn't believe how far our country had come from when I was fifteen. Every time I saw a LOVE WINS T-shirt, I misted. That basement wood shop seemed eons away and the acid of that jock's words relegated to sawdust.

My only complaint was that there was zero food. Like, nada. Okay, there was *one* sad falafel stand that looked disgusting. And like my dad always says, "Falafel makes you feel awful." I shall add another: "Shawarma has bad karma." As in, callin' the Kaopectate. Needless to say, rotating mystery meat was not in the game for my innards, and mid-bitch sesh, Marcello stopped me, saying, "Child. We only eat ice chips and drink alcohol. I have not had a carb in months, child." And so with that, we decided our perfect rainbow *giornata* had to fade to black so Momma could get some fucking pasta. We walked off, hearing the dulcet tones of Ariana Grande, who I thought, until that day, was a font. We found ourselves at nearby Locande Verde, chowing, when the fireworks began—bright bursts of more colors as a vivid noisy exclamation point to a weekend of bliss kicked off by SCOTUS and ending with couples leaving the piers, streaming in hordes by the large window of the restaurant, arm in arm, and singing.

WORST WEDDING DATE, BEST MARRIAGE

My parents met Labor Day weekend of 1971 and were married the day after Christmas. Yes, December 26. Just so bizarre. My grandfather Frank Kopelman said it would be a tax benefit, truth be told, they had that *When Harry Met Sally* . . . thing going of "When you want to spend the rest of your life with someone, you want the rest of your life to start as soon as possible." Though all the guests showed up with a smile and are grinning merrily in every shot in their wedding album, I am certain they were ripshit to haul ass back from their Christmas vacations to snowy New York *in a blizzard, no less*. But cozy in a hotel ballroom my future parents became husband and wife. My mom was the most beautiful twenty-one-year-old bride and my dad was obsessed with her. Their marriage was the envy of all my friends, who marveled that "Arie and Coco actually love each other."

As I grew up and swooned over this guy or that one, professing love after five minutes, my parents would say, "Slow down! You don't *love him*, you don't even know him!" My heart-eyeballed defense was always reminding them of their apparently shotgun wedding (it wasn't), and my dad said in our old kitchen at 45 East Sixty-sixth Street, "If you *ever* do what we did, I will kill you." They got lucky. They made it, but so many of their friends did not. One piece of sterling advice my mom gave me, when I asked what made them last, was to not do what I call the creepy Hamptons marriage, where the mom has the loaded SUV outside on the last day of school and schleps to [insert summer community]

aric
+
coco

12·26·71

with the kids till Labor Day and the husband pops up on the Crampton Shitney or commuter airline on the weekends. My folks always stayed together. Not because she feared my dad would bang (but, believe me, I have seen *many* mice playing while the cat's away) but because she didn't want to ever get used to being apart. They're best friends and somehow stuck it out.

One of the best quotes I've ever heard about marital longevity was from the late great Bruce Paltrow, legendary producer and father of Gwyneth, who admitted that his amazing marriage to actress Blythe Danner endured because "We never wanted to get divorced at the same time." It was so honest and incredible to hear, because I grew up in such a bubble, believing marriage was perfect and some sort of fairy tale.

Harry and I bicker about all kinds of crazy shit (texting at the wheel, bringing business to the dinner table), but the times I've come closest to calling Raoul Felder and filing for a D have all evolved around "adventure."

The most memorable was when Harry led me down an Aspen trail called AMF. My husband is an insanely gifted skier, having raced on a development team. He was cut from the Olympic trials but skied professionally for the United States on an International Ski Federation team in Europe for two years, which is why he was practically a senior citizen when he graduated college. The day in question, we went to the top of Snowmass and switched to the pommel lift up to the tippity top, and I blindly followed him down the trail against my better judgment. It was a *cliff* of waist-high powder and I started to panic. I quote unquote "engaged my core" slash "powerhouse" and worked impossibly hard to turn my quivering legs. I was in *waaaaaay* over my head. I thought, *Holy fucking shit, this could not be worse.* And then, like in a movie when someone says that and then lightning strikes and torrential rain pours down, the cliff gave way to a forest, where I had to thread the steep needle of the narrow trail through trees. I was positive I'd go the way of Sonny Bono and screamed, *"I fucking hate you!"* Despite the twenty-degree winds, I was sweating like a pig. Make that a pig in a ski suit. Two more hairpin turns and I wiped out and fell. I burst into tears and I was aching in every muscle in my body. *"I want a divorce! I am serious!"* Harry was laughing and coached me how to get down. Livid, I finally made it down and stormed by him, red-faced and tearstained. When a friend's husband saw us inside and I told him Harry had idiotically made me ski something called AMF, he looked like the Edvard Munch painting *The Scream.* "You know what that stands for, right?" he asked. "'Adios, motherfucker.'" Nice.

I called my parents, bawling that I hated my husband, and they laughed and talked me down, saying they adored him and to give him a break—he never would've done it on purpose. I got over it with a glass of red wine, and naturally now we laugh about it. But the point is that my parents guided and supported our marriage. Not just by example, but also with sage advice and patient talks. They took our children so we could get away for the weekend; they sat with me and played during what is to most people Happy Hour but to moms can be Suicide Hour, assisting in bath time, stories, and bedtime. I could not have gotten through those early years of child-rearing without them.

When my kids were nine, six, and five, my parents celebrated their fortieth wedding anniversary. My brother, Willie, and I decided that since they didn't want a party to celebrate, we would (tough shit) throw them a surprise party. With our spouses in cahoots, we cajoled them to a "wine tasting" and ambushed them with all their friends at our favorite little restaurant in Sun Valley, Cristina's, the homiest nook you can imagine—a small cabin with a roaring fire and delicious cooking smells from the crackling kitchen. It was a truly special night; here is the toast Willie and I took turns reading:

> 'Twas the night after Christmas
> And all over the world
> Vacations were ruined
> As a marriage unfurled.
>
> Dad loved Mom's suede clogs
> And her accentless French.
> She loved his sharp wit
> And knew he was a mensch.

When Mom and Dad met
Dad wore a red plaid blazer.
Vegas odds had placed bets,
But amazingly its ugliness did not faze her.

But Dad won her heart,
For underneath was a humorous charm.
His humor was brilliant
Even if his Belgian Shoes were cause for alarm.

The engagement was so short
The bridal atelier thought Mom was knocked up.
But why wait to wed
When your heart's all locked up?

'Twas a date inconvenient,
With weather egregious,
But it was so warm and cozy
Within the St. Regis.

The groom was a riot,
The bride was a hottie.
Soon my brother and I arrived,
Sometimes nice, mostly naughty.

They dealt with mice, stress, and chaos,
With kids and drunk clients,
And those awful teen years
Met with 'tude and defiance.

You put up with my boyfriends
And never kvetched,
And now you have Sadie
And Ivy and Fletch!

There are no more devoted grandparents
Than Poppy Arie and Grammy Coco.
Jill hands over the tots
When they drive her quite loco.

My morbid 'rents just bought funeral plots
Side by side on Nantucket.
It's a little weird and creepy
But they think Queens cemeteries suck it.

So raise a glass to forty years
And here's to loving your spouse.
To us, we're Daffer Dan, Frog Friend,
Polar Bear Cub, and Miss Mouse.

We love celebrating you
And we're having a blast.
You guys have proven
That true love will always last. . . .

WE LOVE YOU!
THANKS FOR BEING THE BEST PARENTS EVER!

Now together almost forty-four years, the duo are happier than ever, doting on five grandchildren and traveling through their golden years in such a blissful partnership. This book would have zero pages if it weren't for them, since they both instilled every iota of humor in my brother and me. And while the rest of the country is experiencing holiday postpartum depression and returning gifts the day after Christmas, we are clinking glasses and reveling in their anniversary.

THE KINDERGAUNTLET

For those of you who don't know, school placement in New York City is a fucking war zone. If you don't live in a "good" public school zone (and the "good" schools seem to have little correlation with the "good" neighborhoods), you are totes going through metal detectors. And if you can fork over tuition or swing a scholarship, you might start looking into private schools for your nuggets as early as in utero to get them into a kindergarten of choice. I'm not quite sure how these admissions officers judge the kids, but I guess they can glean a lot from finger-painting, blocks, and sand. Oh, and they fully grill the parents as well, obviously.

We got Sadie (and then Ivy) into an all-girl's private school without too much trouble—only a few bribes, lies, and blow jobs, no big whoop. When we were applying to kindergarten for my son, Fletch, I wished I could shove a wig on him and send him off every morning with Sadie and Ivy, but, alas, we had to start fresh and try to jam him into one of the coveted fifty private spots with a thousand kids competing. We didn't want to move, and I wasn't about to pull a Sally Field and bone some fat bespectacled board of ed. dude (a scene that makes me forever recall that sad movie *Forrest Hump*).

So we cast our net wide, touring the city for the right place for Fletch. We visited campuses and considered the options. I filled out the applications and wrote the obligatory essays, something we hadn't had to do for the girls' school. The whole process chipped away at our sanity a little, but I'm happy to report that for the most part we held our shit together, even knowing that most other competing families were hiring writing coaches—moonlighting PhDs and novelists, for fuck's sake—to "massage" their personal statements. We didn't need Xanax to get through it like some others I know, but it's still daunting to sum up your five-year-old in a one-page "Parents' Statement." In the end I managed to painstakingly construct something I must admit I was rather proud of. We were a good package! I was feeling pretty confident.

But then Fletch's nursery school director made a comment that sent my blood pressure into the stratosphere. I became one of *those moms.*

"Mrs. Kargman, you know we love you, but . . . the boys' schools are different from the girls' schools. Much, much, *much* more conservative."

I gulped. "So?"

"So we appreciate your irreverent side, and that worked with the girls' school, as Thérèse is very downtown and open." (She was our East Village–dwelling admissions director at the girls' school.)

"And . . ."

"And we would advise that you cover up your tattoos during these interviews."

Shock.

I think my quiet—stone-cold disbelief is what it was—made Harry start talking. "Totally, totally," he said. I continued to stare in stunned silence until our little meeting was done.

Out on the street I threw a hissy fit of hear-me-roar proportions. I admit it, I acted like a big baby, or actually more like a snippy righteous teenager trying to "be herself." I was going all Whitney Houston about being who I am, when Harry very calmly said, "Sweetie. No one is trying to change you. They're simply saying that this is a very uptight scene and to play the game! It's really not a big deal and you're being crazy."

Well. Nothing makes a woman go crazier than being told she is crazy. My rants escalated from the "Greatest Love of All" to Heart's "Barracuda."

"I AM WHO I AM AND FUCK THESE ROBOTIC VA-NILLA FUCKING SCHOOLS AND THEIR DEMONIC GATEKEEPERS!"

Harry calmly explained that no one was attacking me. Or him. They were just looking out for Fletch. Was I seriously going to cut off my nose to spite my face if it would affect our kid? he asked.

Ugh, fine. Pop my anger balloon. Deflate my righteousness. He had a point. I agreed I'd wear long sleeves to cover my wrists, NBD.

The date rolled around for the first interview. And, just my luck, it was 98 degrees. And, like the boy band of that temperature, it was insuffs. I was shvitzing my balls off before I even got to the corner, and I was in my sleeveless dress, my leather jacket draped over my shoulder. When we walked in, I put the jacket on to cover the ink on my wrists. Everyone else was wearing short sleeves and here I was, dressed for Halloween on an Africa-hot day. I felt and looked like a complete asshole.

But I managed to smile as I shook hands with the pretty blond admissions director. She was reed thin, stylish, and perfectly sweat free. She led us up the stairs on a tour, and with each step I felt the sweat gathering at my temples and dripping down my body. My pits were a swamp of caked Tom's of Maine lavender deodorant and faucetlike perspiration. I was almost seeing stars when we got to the ninth-floor gym and I thought I was going to pass out. We went into the interview, were seated on a lovely set-tee, and discussed my little guy. I remember sitting up straight and politely answering a stream of questions, what sports he en-joys, what toys, what a typical Saturday consists of. And that sweat was pouring out of every pore. We left a total of ninety minutes later and burst into the street, me peeling off my now soaked-through jacket. It was so BO-logged that I almost needed to trash it so as not to be picked up by Homeland Security for possession of chemical weaponry. I could've bottled it and shipped it to ISIS and we'd win the War on Terror. My hair was so matted and gnarlissssimi I was mortified, and my whole being was like that Charlie Brown smelly kid with squiggly lines orbiting him to connote stink. Good times!

Thankfully, the rest of the tours were mercifully cooler and my various blazers and leather jackets were suitable. But here was the problem: our first-choice school was the one where I had looked like I was mid menopausal hot flash and probably behaved like a fucking lunatic who had to catch her breath and wipe per-spiration every twenty seconds.

Fast-forward two months. The setting was SoulCycle, aka spinagogue. I was going bonkers as a shut-in during Hurricane Sandy, and women were dangling off the ceiling, cramming their way to the desk, begging for a spare bike, since our kids had been home all week because of the weather. I did a hope dance, which is when I cross my fingers and do a goofy jig, and it somehow worked! I was given one of the bikes in the Staten Island/ undesirable section in the back. Ordinarily I'm a front-row type, so I'm right up in the action, but that day I was so desperate that I was still fired up to be in Siberia—I was going to finally move my ass and get out all my pent-up aggression from being cooped up.

I banged my hip bone on every bike on my way to the nose-bleed section up on risers in the back corner, put my water in the water holder, and blissfully started setting up my bike. And then. All the blood suddenly drained out of my face as I looked at the ringed hand putting water in the water holder next to me. It was the pretty blond admissions director from my first-choice school—the very one where I had been sweating my balls off and panting like a golden retriever. Fucklesby McShitcock. I was there in a black ribbed tank top that said "I ❤ STACEE JAXX" from *Rock of Ages.* That would be Tom Cruise's drug addict character who had two life-size gun tattoos on either side of his pelvis pointed at his (probably pierced) cock. And, of course, my own tattoos—sweet little ribbons tied into bows on the inside of my wrists—were obviously exposed. Awesome. I got on the bike and kept my head down but knew she saw me. My mind was racing, thoughts going something like this:

Okay, I can do this. In a few minutes the lights will go off. It will be pitch-black. She is here to work out, she isn't doing research. She meets thousands of parents and she doesn't know who I am.

But wait . . . she doesn't know who I am . . . we are all faceless, names piling up in a tower of files. Maybe if I say hi I could imprint myself on her memory?

"Listen," I said leaning over to her, "my preschool director told me not to show any of you my tattoos, so I was totally sweating to death the day of our interview because it was deathly hot

♥ ♡

and I was wearing a leather jacket!" I showed her both wrists guiltily, then started pretending I was Wonder Woman with her power cuffs with full sound effects, and she started laughing. "Oh well!" I shrugged guiltily.

"I can't believe they said that." She laughed, shaking her head. "But don't worry, Jill—don't tell anyone, but I have one, too." And with that, the lights went out and Madonna rang through the air.

www.Holyshit.com/FUCKYEAH!

I came home and triumphantly announced that I owned it, as Harry smiled and put his head in his hands. I was incorrigible. Oh, and Fletch got in. While he is a smart cookie and maybe would have pulled it off, I maintain that back row interaction was a key factor.

I think when he applies to college, I'm gonna get sleeved.

THINGS I HATE THAT EVERYONE ELSE LOVES

Cake

If you're asking yourself "Who the fuck doesn't like cake?" you are like many a birthday party hostess when I was a kid. It got so I would sob on the way to each and every birthday party, tearfully imploring my mom, "Tell the mother I don't want cake! Tell the mother!" I needed her to help me avoid the angry, DEFCON 2, *"You don't want cake?* What do you mean you don't want cake? Try it! Just take a bite, it's so delicious!" I didn't want to take a bite. Because I fucking hate cake. To this day I decline cake, because I find it too sweet and I don't like the texture. I love chocolate and ice cream and have a goddamn soul, I just don't like cake. So sorry.

· · ·

Summer

As annoying people love to say, "I can't even." Every June I start to feel like a motherfucking mogwai, shrouded in shadow, yelling, "Bright light! Bright light!" And yet I am forced to inhabit the world, and like Robert Pattinson's diamondy chest outside that Volturi castle, it doesn't go well. I am not only an insta-lobster but also miz from heat and, the cherry on top, I had melanoma six years ago. Oh, and don't get me started on fat peoples' midriffs and toes that go over the edge of their flip-flops. Summer—no thanks.

The beach

See above. But more specifically, the whole sand-in-vagina thing is so unpleasant I just want to boil myself. I try to take a walk, but that shit is a pedicure ruiner. I try to sit, but get bored. The second we arrive, I ask if it's lunchtime yet and spend the first hour waiting to crack open the sandwiches from their prison of tinfoil. Then I'm asking if we can leave yet. Other detractors include: obesity, the smell of sunblock (which I swear is ineffective), screaming children, jellyfish, boats you're not invited on, flying umbrellas that could impale you at any moment, sharks, and drowning people. Other than that, it's great.

A beer

I was handed my first beer at thirteen at a Columbia University party I had no business being at. But since someone had handed it to me in a classic Solo cup and since I understood it to

 be "America's water," I felt I should try that shit. Not even a glitter rainbow cup could make that horse pee taste anything other than dis- queecious. That is my brother's word, which is an exponent of disgusting. Yes, I wanted to be cool, but not that badly. I left it on some kid's desk.

When I was in high school, I went to an off-campus party and I thought I'd give beer a second try, since I was at a real live keg- ger like real American youth! Gnar. Ly. And that's it, folks! Never again; it's an acquired taste that this beeyotch simply won't ac- quire and I'm aiiight with that. So please don't tell me there's nothing better after a ski run—it ain't happenin'. #cowpiss #trashtastic #daterape #sports #thegame #yuck.

Rap and also country-western

I am aware I'm losing more of you as this list progresses, but I hear honesty is the best policy and so I've just got to tell you I'm just a rock 'n' roll girl! I love guitars! Oh, and show tunes! (I am Andrew Lloyd Webber's bitch.) What can I say? I like the occa- sional rap song when there is a sampled rock song in the back- ground, or when it's Lin-Manuel Miranda-y with awesome melodies, but that's pretty much it. Don't you dare say that I am racist, because I'm an equal opportunity offender and despise country music even more! No song needs lyrics about screen doors slamming and jilted lovers smashing windshields. I will always be a hard rocker. Sorry, Nashville.

• • •

♡ ♡

Your dog

The final straw for you? I hope we can still be friends. Or maybe not. If you French-kiss your pooch, we probably can't be. And, no, it's not like you saying you hate my kids. My kids aren't licking your vagina when you walk into a room and barking incessantly. Okay, maybe they bark incessantly, but they won't forever! I am a magnet for dog tongues, and while I of course believe in ethical treatment of animals and believe that beast who shot poor Cecil the lion should rot in a Namibian jail, that doesn't mean I want your dog jumping on me and covering my all-black outfit with golden retriever fur. Once I was at an ATM, taking out money to pay the painter/extortionist, and the next thing I know, this dog is jumping up on me on hind legs and licking me. The owner was blithely taking out her fat wad of cash, unawares. When I nicely said something like "Um, ma'am, I'm so sorry, but your dog is, like, on me," she acted like I should be so lucky and took her dog, saying, "Come on, honey, let's get you away from that mean, mean lady." Bitch. And BITCH!

I AM THE LORD OF THE LORD OF THE RINGS

Here's a weird fun fact about me: I hate Hollywood futuristics and I hate Hollywood make-believes. I hate flying things that are not airplanes. I hate wizards. I hate capes. I hate powers. I hate swords that glow. I haaaaaate dragons.

But the *Lord of the Rings* trilogy, which features all of the above and then some? I am *obsesssssed*. I could watch the movies five hundred times and still want to watch them in full when I stumble upon one of them on TNT. Each time is like the first time. I drool with excitement.

The real first time was actually the premiere of the first movie. Harry is a total fan—he'd been counting the days to opening night like those blond-dreadlocked lunatics who camp outside the Apple store. I'm pretty sure he jerks off to the books, and he was so euphoric to score those tickets I just had to go.

When the lights went down in the Ziegfeld, the look on his

face was happier than on our wedding day. Fuck, I should've brought a flask. This was going to be the seventh circle of Beelzebub's bubbling lava pits of infernal hell.

And then I heard the spine-tingling tones of genius Cate Blanchett's powerful, soothing voice. She gave us the backstory of man's hubris and greed, and explained how the ages had passed as the ring slept in the murky waters of layers of time. I was, oddly, shockingly, lured. Big-time. The coming scenes reeled me in further, though the happy Shire shit was second for me to the spooky elements connoting impending doom. The darkness of that flaming vagina thing and Mordor's blackened Gothic gates turned me on almost as much as Viggo's blue eyes.

(*Note:* We interrupt this broadcast to clarify that this rhapsodic panty wringer is for *Lord of the Rings* EXCLUSIVELY and not, I repeat *not*, about the prequel trilogy of *The Hobbit.* That is categorically different and not in this league and the cast is entirely made up of eye broccoli. And now back to our regularly scheduled programming of jazzing over *LOTR.*)

So, Veegs. I mean.

In a word: smoldering. Liv Tyler, already genetic lottery winner, hit extra jackpot getting to play tonsil hockey with Aragorn. My boner was longer than Liv's fairy fingers, or, as JAPs say, "I die." He had it going on with his armor and with his sword (no, not that one) and honor and bravery and hairstyle. Oh, and, PS, he could've totally boned that pretty blond princess 'cause his pointy-eared gal pal was on her way to those ghost ships to Neverland, but he totes didn't. Unicorn! Instead he touched that Art Nouveau necklace charm gifted by his love, who could make halfling-saving potions out of weeds. For the record, I would've wished they had Cathy Waterman design something a tad more chic, like Charlize's cray crowns and rings and shit in *Snow White and the Huntsman*, but I say bygones, yo.

And even though the vile fucked-up melted ogre-like Orcs still haunt my dreams, I have heart palps when I remember or see those ladders leaning against the fortress wall, or the battering ram with a flaming wolf mouth at the head. But thank goodness for those green-ghosty pirate peeps lurking in that mountain crevasse that scared the horsies shitless as they bucked and whinnied their way out of their posts. That ruled. Sorry to be Beavis and Butt-head over here *but it did.* And in the end, who doesn't adore a kiss as a bow at the Hollywood ending. I sure as hell do. So if there are any of you who haven't seen it—and therefore whom I have completely lost with my homage to this genius in celluloid form, do yourself a favor and on the next blizzardy January sick day, when you're sniffling and miz and holed up, and binge watch all three. It will be penicillin for your soul. At the risk of sounding like a frat boy with a limited vocab, I daresay it is epic.

SOCIAL MEDIA TIPS

what NOT to post!

Selfies on private jets

Guys, make it stop. Like, seriously. So happy for you that you're firin' up the bird, but need you post dasshit? Doing so smacks of insecurity. And besides, the people who actually *own* private jets keep them private; it's the renters who post. And, by the way, we can tell by the oval windows that you're on a private plane. You don't need to zoom out to be sure to capture the wide interior and leather seats. We get it. You're fabulous. Knock it off! #braggart

Publicly thanking Valentino for that time on his yacht

It's always nice to instagram a thanks to a hostess for a backyard BBQ or cozy dinner party, but a tabletop shot with caviar and black-tie waitstaff? Public thanks is a tricky one—sometimes it's genuine gratitude to the host, and other times it's pretty clear you're bragging. I'm sure it was fun to be invited to an event that's harder to get into than Fort Knox, but see above. Cut the shit.

Food you just made

Unless you have published a cookbook, we really don't care about your caprese salad. Yes, it's nice to know people are still making things and that is so nice for your kids that you prepare delicious meals rather than heat up ready-made from Citarella (ahem), but it's not only mildly smug to show us your culinary masterpieces but also boring. Special mention for über-perfect kids' birthday cakes. If you want to share a botched Elmo, I love you. Duncan Hines with a Ninjago cake topper, go for it. But if you get off on fondant-covered wedding-worthy cakes for a toddler only so you can show what a virtuoso frosting artist you are, it makes us all feel like lazy losers. Which we are, but no need to squeeze lemon juice.

Your pets doing dumb shit

Is that your cat in your husband's hoodie? Oh, you silly goose! Your dog throwin' shade with a frown and a caption that reads No More Mister Nice Guy! Isn't that just the cutest? No, I'm not amused. I know *you are*, because you've owned and raised him since puppyhood and know his every darling move, but you are likely the only one squealing with delight over that punim.

Outfit options in a full-length mirror

Nothing says teen girl before a night out like a body shot in front of a door mirror. This is totally fine to do *privately*—like in a text to one person—if you need advice. But sharing your pre-game outfits online? So odd! We all like to blast music and get ready for a night out, but it's so awks to take that fun, private moment alone or with a few friends and make it public. Also your phone is blocking part of you. And you look so serious. If you really need to do it, at least own it with a smile.

Happy eight-month birthday to my baby who can't read

I know, your "heart is exploding" and you didn't know you "could love like this." That's great! And it's for your family and friends, but when you address your comments to the kid directly, it's weird. He or she is an infant and will not be able to see or respond to that post. All that said, I will admit that I understand the impulse on this faux pas. I wrote thank you notes as Sadie after she was born. *But I did not make them public.*

THERE ONCE WAS
A GAL FROM NANTUCKET

To most people, Nantucket is a caricature of preppiness: whale-patterned pants, perky blondes, and lobster rolls. It's true that it's very much Aryan Nation time out there. There are barely any people of color, and we Kopelman/Kargmans are part of the few-Jew club. In point of fact, there is a synagogue on the island. Sure, it's in the basement of a church. And they sell whalebone mezuzahs and Nantucket red *kippot*, with embroidered navy whales around the perimeter. But still.

We first started visiting Nantucket as a family when I was little.

We'd take the two-and-a-half-hour ferry ride from Cape Cod, and I was intrigued to watch all the over-the-rail vomiters. I definitely felt out of place, like Wednesday Addams in a place where Lilly Pulitzer herself had vomited on the entire population. But I loved the long walks; the simple food; and, most of all, the unique time-warpy, quirky character of the island. We returned every year right before school started, when my dad could take off work, renting a home each time.

When I was a freshman in college, however, my parents said they'd decided to buy a place—a small historic house built in 1790. Cool fact: Nantucket has a greater concentration of historic homes than any other place in this country. Talk about the epitome of time warp!

My dad is a fanatical preservationist, so when we did some work on the house, he had his godson, Johnny, who is a blacksmith in Pennsylvania, make every nail so that the hardware was in synch with 1790 building materials. Semi-psycho, but supercool.

"We're going for Thanksgiving," said my dad. That was a month away.

"Thanksgiving? But I want to go home!" I was constantly homesick for the city and couldn't stand the thought of not getting my parade fix.

But my protests yielded nothing. We went to the Rock, or what I called Preppy Alcatraz, on the most frigid day ever. I had never been in the off-season, and here I was, on my favorite holiday, in a brand-new house.

But it was heaven. Arctic tundra heaven, but heaven. The thickest fog I have ever seen outside of a Tim Burton movie rolled down our street. It looked like you could touch it. Willie and I used to make fun of the dude from the tour outfit who dressed up in a ye olde toppe hatte and led mainland morons on a tour of island suicides and murders: Pilgrim spirits stuck in limbo on the whale oil capital of the Eastern Seaboard. But with the fog and the emptiness of the streets, that was the moment when I started to understand the appeal of those tours.

The day after our turkeyfest, we were told to gather on Main

Street for the tradition of hot spiced wine, apple cider, and next-holiday-anticipatory caroling. We followed the hordes of people in thick wool sweaters, scarves, and earmuffs. I felt a tad like I was off to Gobbler's Knob in *Groundhog Day,* and I was Jill Murray, a bitter curmudgeon who thought the holidays were getting a little overdone. But, like Bill, I melted despite the cold. All my grinchiness evaporated as I saw little apple-cheeked children running up and down the evergreen- and lantern-lined, cobblestoned street. The whole town counted down from ten in unison, and then the mayor pressed a button and tiny twinkling Christmas lights illuminated the entire street of trees. It was absosmurfly amazing. I instantly became a Who in Whoville rather than a grimacing Grinch. I sang my heart out and decided we would always go back for Thanksgiving.

As the years passed, I had several ups and downs and retreated, often in October and November, to the island. Once after a bad breakup, I went alone. I was also training to walk the New York marathon (one of the coolest things I've ever done, BTdubs), so went out one day to walk to 'Sconset, the tiny dot of a town on the opposite side of the island. I came home and was so freaked by the howling wind that I slept with the TV on. Not that I truly thought a cleaver-toting dug-up Christopher Walken look-alike would hatchet me to death, but loneliness + time warp = nightmares.

Now I go with my own kids, and while they love it for normal-person reasons—surf, sand, and ice cream—I will always love the goth side. I actually think Tim Burton needs to shoot a movie there in the winter. Until then, I'll walk the winding, tiny stone streets in the rain, filming the cobalt sky for the haunted film sequence in my mind.

EVEN SUPERMODELS
SING THE BLUES

At a dinner party last summer, I was seated, *avec* calligraphed place card, next to some dude I didn't know. But he saw someone at another table—an old friend he just had to catch up with—and so switched his wife into his place next to me. She was a supermodel. I'm not exaggerating. I'm not just trying to communicate that she was gorgeous. And she was not a model who calls herself a supermodel, she was a bona fide, million-Twitter-followers legit supermodel.

Unfazed, I introduced myself, and I was pleasantly surprised to find she was quite intelligent. Her work from a very young age (she'd been dropped off in New York to make her own way at fifteen!) had exposed her to countless international editors, photographers, designers, artists, and fashion clients, and it showed. She was truly a citizen of the world, and I was impressed.

We started talking kiddies and she told me how she had opted for a water birth with no epidural. I find that cray but, as Ali G would say, *respeck*. I certainly couldn't handle that pain and personally wanted my epidural put in as soon as possible—in the fucking parking lot wouldn't have been too early. I joked with her how my gyno told me to wait four to six weeks before exercise or "intercourse," which became "six to eight weeks," when I relayed the news to Harry. The elegant mannequin threw her head back in laughter and I'd have sworn I'd seen the same effortless giggle in a Mario Testino snap. Then she opened up to match my postpartum guilty admission.

"When my child was about two weeks old, I walked into the bathroom and my husband was . . ." She curled her hand and mimed him jerkin' the gherkin. Nervously, I looked over at him, drunk, dumb, and happy with his ol' pal, while I was now picturing him as Donald Trump firing his apprentice. But she continued. "I burst into tears and could not stop crying because he cheated on me!"

I paused. Huh? Everyone knows all men help put Mr. Kleenex's kids through college forever!

"Are you kidding? He's not cheating on you. He's fiddling the flesh flute!" I said, laughing. "It's not like it was someone else's hand, it was attached to his arm!"

"No," she said firmly. "It's cheating."

"It's completely normal!" I protested, defending her horny husband. "It's so not cheating! It's just hand-to-gland combat."

"I was simply devastated," she said, wincing at the memory of his soapy schwantz through the shower glass. "I told him NEVER, EVER to do that thing again. I made him promise."

I was so thrown and had never heard of such a thing! Didn't she hear guys discussing the five-knuckle shuffle at every turn? And then I realized, maybe not. Men probably changed the way they spoke around her, and she hadn't picked up on the fact that masturbation is most dudes' favorite pastime. I thought everyone knew that. So commonplace is it that I hadn't even been surprised to hear that in the U.S. Navy the sailors are taught by the higher-ups how to slice off the top of a cantaloupe, stick it in the micro-wave to warm and soften it, fuck the fruit, and then blow their load in its orangey pulp. Clearly she had not heard this high seas myth. She was more than a little horrified.

"Listen, every guy on earth high fives with Yul Brynner, that's par for the course," I went on. "It's natural."

"But he is married to *me*!"

Ah. Lightbulb. Gotcha. Every other guy on earth must be married to trolls like me. Or fat aging housewives who wear asex-ual pleat-front jeans and tapestry vests, not haute couture. Rules were different in her rarefied world, it seems.

If I had cared just a little bit more, I might have continued the conversation and educated her to the fact that all guys—even guys who are married to supermodels—whack it to someone else. Maybe another supermodel. And, yes, maybe all other guys whack it to her, but if her hubby can schtupp her, naturally his mind will drift to her catwalking comrades sometimes! I mean, really, variety is the spice of life and should be embraced!

And I might have told her something I learned from a male coworker many years ago. We'd had a department lunch and were walking down the street back from the restaurant. A model walked by with no bra, and her nips were showing through her blouse as her boobs bobbed. All the dudes' eyeballs popped out as if animated by Looney Tunes, and their tongues rolled out like a Hollywood red carpet. I grimaced—they were acting like ani-mals, almost panting even. A coworker noticed my disgust.

"Don't worry, Jill," he consoled me with a hand on my shoul-der. "For every hot girl you see, there's a guy who's tired of fuck-ing her."

♡ ♡

This insight into men's minds was very revelatory. I marveled at his candor and actually in that moment changed the way I thought about monogamy. If models can't be the sole joystick maneuverer of their husbands' dicks, how the hell could I? It actually totally released me from jealousy and stress. And if I ever walked in while my husband had a shower date with Palmela Handerson, I wouldn't care! With three kids, if I had to bang every second he wanted to, I'd be exhausted. That supermodel may be unusually smart, but she was dumb to bust in while the shower was going.

BEES IN MY BONNET

end of summer edition!

"Where did you summer?"

It's the same thing every September. I want to get T-shirts made that say MINE WAS FINE. HOW WAS YOURS? *Enough* with the torturous default travel-flaunting small talk; I already *saw* on your Insta that you flew privately to Capri, then hopped on Valentino's yacht! So shut up about it. When people smarmily ask me *where I summered,* I blithely respond, "DURITO!" They look a little confused, assuming it must be the new It island floating in some far-flung time zone, and ask, "Oh, yes . . . Isn't there's a new Aman resort there?" I correct them: "Nope. DURITO is where I live in New York City: Down Under Roosevelt Island Tram Overpass. That's where I *summer.*" That shuts them up. They bite their lower lips and give me a look of pity, like I spent Julaugust opening fire hydrants with a wrench and dancing in the stream of water or joining in a rat conga line down Madison, kicking tumbleweeds out of my way with my not-Louboutins. VOM people. And stop using *summer* as a verb!

Awky fall hooves

New season, new shoes! Just *please* get the kind that you wear, not ones that *wear you*. I saw a socialite at a fashion show who was teetering on quasi stilts that made Lady Gaga look barefoot—a platform with no heel, which left her unbalanced and awkward looking rather than confident and sexy. You can't strut on stilts unless you know how to rock them! It has to be comfy or you'll look like a ridickity donk doofus. I'm also not a fan of boots with toes peeping out—WTF is a toeless boot for? If it's cold enough for boots,

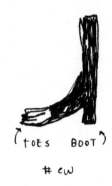

(↑ toes   boot)

cw

I shouldn't see your toes popping out. I like shoes, don't get me wrong. But nothing you put on your feet should make you walk like a drunk, hobbled giraffe.

The incessant barrage of back-to-school commercials

Jesus fucking Christ with the backpacks and the pencil cases and the tiny cargo shorts! I have news for you, JC motherfuckin' Penney, if you would curtail some of the model children in slow-mo skipping to school, I would be forever grateful. Oh, and by the way, maybe don't start unleashing the floor *the first week of July*. Please, we just got to summer, yo! Last year, I saw back-to-school commercials *before* Toyotathon's Fourth of July sale ads. Amazon spammed me at midnight on June 30! Sheesh. I even got a Halloween costume e-blast in August. People are insane.

• • •

Humble brags

I recognize that this is an oxymoron. However, the New Bragging is always couched in an eye roll or reframed with something being a *big old drag*. *Por ejemplo: Ugh, the traffic to Teterboro is just getting worse and worse!* Or, *I'm so stressed overseeing the gut job on Park Avenue and the renovation in Southampton! Presiding over two sets of blueprints was like a full-time job this summer!* In both cases, the complainer is expressing dismay over things other peeps (including myself) would kill for. Clearly you're loaded and doing the backstroke in a new pool filled with gold coins if you carry your two blueprint scrolls like a yoga mat. Don't whine about your *insanely busy summer* and needing a vacation from your vacation. Your *life* is a vacation compared to the rest of the planet, beeyotch!

People who crack out their winter duds when it's still sweltering

Q. What did one mink say to the other mink?

A. See you at synagogue.

Believe me, no one is more thrilled to switch from sandals to tights and boots and crack out the winter outerwear, but sometimes people get too zealous, sporting furs when it's still 50 degrees out. Slow down, people—you in cahoots with the back-to-school commercial people, or what?! So thrilled you dig your duds, but let's wait till the mercury plummets a bit more, yes? Of course, the reverse is also common come May, when it can still be freezing out and some women break out their strappy slingbacks while it's cold enough to still warrant thigh-high black leather shitkickers.

"This summer just flew by!"

No, it didn't. It inched. Time is all relative, and if you experience it as whizzing by, what really is the point of comparing notes on it? Emoji of the boar followed by the ring. The other thing is that the same people who complain that it's freezing in the winter then complain that it's so hot in the summer. They're called seasons, people! If you don't like them, move to the desert where it's always the same. I for one, as we know, welcome Halloween and am more than thrilled to see all those bright colors go b-bye. Black is the new orange. . . .

WELCOME TO THE JUNGLE

When I heard all these parents going shithouse over Lenore Skenazy, the author of *Free-Range Kids*, allowing her nine-year-old son to ride the subway by himself, I wondered what they'd say about my parents. If her kid was an organic wandering chicken, I was a wild turkey—I started taking the public bus to school at *eight*. Keep in mind two key things: (1) *There were no cellphones*, and (2) Poor Etan Patz had *just* vanished the year before. But that didn't stop them! They didn't seem to be negligent parents—as crazy as that sounds—because Kathryn Wender came with me, and on our M101 rides we ran into half our friends. It was normal! Even though the city was a cesspool filled with muggings back then. But I guess I was lucky.

When I turned nine, I started getting an allowance, I think five clams a week. I saved up and took my bus pass and announced I was headed out to Tower Records on the West Side. No one cared. My mom grew up on the West Side, so she didn't think anything of it, but in the early eighties I can tell you it was not as safe feeling as the East Side. Aside from our trips to Lincoln Center and to Fairway, I hadn't wandered around that much. But every few weeks, I took the M66 to Tower and blew my ducats on vinyl records, which I played, ladies and gentlemen, on a Fisher-Price record player.

I started out loving First Wave. Yaz, Duran Duran, and Violent Femmes were among my first records. I was glued to MTV, already watching *120 Minutes*, and when hair metal bands started coming on, I became infatuated. Thank goodness I hadn't been older or I would've probably hopped a Greyhound to LA and tried to bang those guyliner lions.

Crazily enough, I can trace my interest in rock to *The Muppet Show*. My nights in 1983 consisted of eating dinner in front of Kermie and the gang, on these cool faux-burl TV tables. Of all the episodes, and I believe I have seen them all, the Alice Cooper one had the biggest effect on me. I was intoxicated by the monster costumes and smoke and guitars. The dark lights and the raccoon eyes made me obsessed. Synth turned to face-melting guitar riffs, and Toto's "Africa" (which I still love) was replaced by Def Leppard. My pilgrimages to Tower became more frequent and I would beg for extra money for doing chores or demand a fifty-cent bribe every time my parents dragged us into an antiques store, which was frequently. I saved and scrounged and my album collection piled up. I played air guitar in the mirror to Foreigner's "Juke Box Hero" (long before the video game), blared Journey, and had to wring out my Calvins when I first saw the Scorpions' album cover for *Love at First Sting*. It had a woman with black hair with side boob showing as she smashed against her motorcycle-jacketed lover, who was devouring her neck, as a tattoo needle perforated the skin of her upper thigh. I would stare at it for what seemed like hours. I still find it to be the sexiest album cover of all time. I was dying to be embraced like that—his leather jean–covered legs encircling her as he gave her a love bite. I wanted to *be her.*

DZON'T GET ME STAHTID about the release of *Appetite for Destruction.* When Guns N' Roses burst onto the scene, my brother and I went apoplectic. I was *obsesssssed,* and it may have been the single album that cemented my cultlike adoration of rock and loathing of almost everything else. I wasn't so crazy about the liner notes illustration of the raped waitress with the panties around her ankles with the violator monster slinking off (in fact, I had nightmares about it), but I wore that record down until I needed a new one. Not to make Metallica fans' heads explode, but the songs I liked were actually the melodic ones like "The Unforgiven" and "Nothing Else Matters," whereas the OTT throttle of other anthems was too much pummeling for me and lacked the rich haunted soul—I think I went through menopause during "Master of Puppets," and only played it for the amazing, rich guitar bridge in the middle.

Years later, when I was writing my first novel, I needed money to pay the bills and freelanced for two years at BMG, Bertelsmann Music Group. They had just acquired Roadrunner Records and I found myself writing "digs"—or description blurbs—for new records from the likes of Screaming Headless Torsos, Fear Factory, Biohazard, and Sepultura. I overused phrases like "blistering riffs," "venomous lyrics," "cookie monster vocals," and "thrashing drum kits."

In the end, though, my work's death metal roster stayed at work, and at home I played more Soundgarden; Alice in Chains; Mother Love Bone; Jane's Addiction; and my all-time favorite band, Nine Inch Nails. Later I turned to splintered regroupings of my old favorites, like Velvet Revolver and Audioslave, and now

I pretty much exclusively play the old music of all the bands I mentioned. Sometimes in a spin class a pop song can puncture my musical vault, but it's rare. To me, no new catchy pop confections can rival the anthems of the first thirty years of my life. Still, I hate when people make obnoxious buzzkilling pronouncements like "Music is dead." There will always be music. I just hope we can get a little more rock back in the radio roster so my kids know more than the nasal-voiced croons of whiny record-company-configured divas. So far, SiriusXM 33 1st Wave and my Pandora eighties rock station are helping turn the tide; recently when Sadie opted for AC/DC over Charli XCX, I felt I was doing something right.

FINDING SALINGER

I came a little close to breaking the law once.

I've never been a particularly big football fan, but I somehow got swept up in the annual Harvard-Yale rivalry. Not so much for the pigskin, or even the tailgating, which I hated—because to me beer tastes like cow piss (not that I've sampled that, but I can imagine)—but for the camaraderie of being on foreign turf, saying hello to fellow navy-clad people I didn't regularly interact with back on campus. It was kind of like meeting an American on vacation abroad and striking up a conversation just because of your shared nationality when you both know you'd never hang Stateside. Plus, Boston obviously has more action than New Haven, so my friends and I went to the game at Harvard every other year, even into our mid-twenties. It was a reunion of sorts.

One year, three years after graduation, my BFF, Vanessa (who is the inspiration for Vanessa on *Odd Mom Out*), and I became absolutely obsessed by a new book called *At Home in the World*, a memoir by Joyce Maynard. It began with her freshman year at

Yale (1973), when *The New York Times Magazine* profiled her for a cover story about being a college student at the time. Maynard rocketed to national attention when her doe-eyed face graced the cover—photo by none other than Richard Avedon—and before long she received reams of fan letters. One of them was from J. D. Salinger.

The literary icon was a notorious recluse, having decided to hole up in New Hampshire and not publish anymore. But that didn't mean he wasn't writing. Joyce wrote him back and a pen pal rapport ensued, followed by a love affair that resulted in her dropping out of Yale and moving to live with him; she was nineteen and he was fifty-three. I don't know what it was about the pairing—perhaps the fact that it was clandestine, more or less, that she kept her silence long after they split up, that she was the mistress and muse of an icon—but Vanessa and I became completely fascinated by her, and all we could do was talk about her memoir. We were a book club with two members, but we told everyone to read it like the gospel. Somehow it captured a time and was a window into the dark world inhabited by this author we had so admired.

So, back to the fall football face-off at Harvard in 1998. Vanessa and I went up to Boston. I was doing magazine work and writing for a dot-bomb and for David Lauren who was launching polo.com, and Vanessa was on her way to becoming the youngest vice president at Young & Rubicam (which she did at twenty-seven). The game ended and everyone was scattering to this party or that bar. We recoiled at some of the familiar faces and didn't feel too social. It was then that Vanessa and I hatched an alternative plan.

Within minutes we bailed from the stadium and were at a car rental. No one really had cellphones and there was no such thing as GPS, so with our Avis map, we made our way up to New Hampshire. We were going to try to meet J. D. Salinger.

HI, WE APPEAR
NORMAL BUT WE
ARE STALKERS

We figured we knew he liked younger women, and while he was by then an old man, perhaps before he died we could somehow befriend him in his small, boring town. Maybe he'd even be our pen pal and give us some treasure trove of manuscripts. Maybe we could just take a picture with him? I bought two of those now-defunct orange cardboard disposable cameras with that crank/wheel thing to rotate the film. It was a pre-Instagram age and those photos were to "share" with each other. The first snap was the sign showing we'd entered Salinger's town of Cornish, New Hampshire. There were no B and Bs around, so we ventured over the state border and into Vermont and found the Juniper Hill Inn. The brochure was printed at Kinko's on pale yellow paper tri-folded, and on the back were Xeroxed photos of the owners' corgis ("our children"). It was getting late, so we decided to grab dinner at a traincar turned diner. Like, an actual one. I got a turkey club with Russian dressing, my typical diner fare with Vanessa in New York. But nothing else about sitting together at a diner was normal. We were out of our element. We were in Kathy Bates/*Misery* rural territory now and were starting to get a little freaked out.

We returned to the hotel after dinner and I went in the phone booth (yes, they still had a phone booth!) and called my now dearly departed, city-dwelling Grandma Ruth to say hi and tell her about our adventure. A part of me also wanted someone on the planet to know where we were in case we disappeared.

"What are you, crazy?" she asked. "You can't be two young girls alone in the wilderness! Just be very careful and remember, not all the nuts are in the nuthouse."

That line has stayed with me always, since I seem to be a five-foot-seven strip of flypaper for lunatics everywhere. In any case, I swore I'd be careful and hung up. In our room, Vanessa and I poured over articles she had harvested about Salinger. We highlighted passages that described the terrain, such as a canopy of foliage or forks in the road. We had earlier noted that he loved Dunkin' Donut holes, so we had procured a box of fifty Munch-kins in one of those friendly boxes with finger slots for convenient carrying. It's amusing now that we were planning to tempt him with mass market pastries as if he were a little kid to be lured by candy to a van, but we figured we "looked normal" and could use them as an icebreaker/offering of some sort. *We come in peace, bearing fried dough, Mr. Salinger!*

The next morning, after our complimentary Continental breakfast, we began our Sherlock Holmesian mission. The town of Cornish was tiny, and the central crossroads of all things Cornish appeared to be the gas pump cum mom 'n' pop convenience store. We sidled up, smiling, and sweetly asked if they knew, by chance, where J. D. Salinger lived.

"WHO'S ASKIN'?" said an old codger in a black-and-red-checked flannel shirt. I want to say he was in overalls, but I might be making that up.

"Uh . . . we are just harmless fans, and—"

"LEAVE 'IM BE!" he grunted.

Vanessa and I turned around with a look on our faces that resembled the emoji with all his teeth in a grimace, like, *sheesh.* No matter. Protective townsfolk, that's all. The pa who ran the show has undoubtedly had his place replaced by a Cumberland Farms or 7-Eleven by now, so there.

With me, map in my hand, as navigator and Vanessa at the wheel, we began to methodically go slo-mo, street by street, on a type of grid, hoping there'd be a mailbox that said SALINGER. No such luck. We continued for an hour, and, gee, I was getting hungry. I'll just take this here one little Munchkin, okay?

No sooner did we crack that fucking Happy Meal–shaped box than I knew poor J.D. would be left with scraps. One became five became ten, which we justified by saying if we actually lined up the doughnut holes in a circle, six would make a doughnut, so we'd really only had a couple of doughnuts each, right? Finally Vanessa forced me to close the container so we would have a few to offer our idol; about twenty sad holes rolled around audibly inside.

We were about to give up when we spied a friendly-looking fella taking a walk. We pulled over and said we were New Yorkers exploring the area, adding a casual "Hey, someone just mentioned that author—Uh, what's his name? Who wrote *Catcher in the Rye?*—lives around this area."

"Oh yeah, sure, right on Saint Gaudens Road."

BIIIIIIIIINGO.

Just like that! We were so chill and at ease, no one would ever think we were *Fatal Attraction* stalkers like Glenn Close. Which is good because we're so not! We just wanted to trespass and invade someone's privacy, that's all!

We circled back to the beginning of the street and went house by house, examining each. Some had swing sets or kiddie tricycles out front—nope. Others had flashier cars, which was so not him. Finally we pulled up to a house that fit every detail of description we could scrounge. The rusty mailbox was unmarked. We both knew this had to be the one. I popped out of the car with the Munchkin box.

Vanessa asked, "What are you going to do?"

"Go knock."

"Wait—what if he calls the police?"

"He won't! We are young, normal girls."

"I don't know about this. . . . Young and Rubicam will fire me if I am arrested." She had a point.

In the end, our life of crime was aborted by a combo of respect for the author and fear of jail. But we somehow felt accomplished just setting eyeballs on what was surely his home. Who knows if he was there or what he was doing, or how many untold novels and short stories sat within that rustic bunker he never left. We took lots of pictures—early selfies—and managed to use up all the film on those cardboard cameras. I later made an album for Vanessa to remember our zany crusade. We may have come home empty-handed in terms of a Salinger sighting, but it was a total *Zen and the Art of Motorcycle Maintenance* adventure, proving the journey is more important than the destination. My best friend and I made a new memory that embodied the kookiness of that moment in time; we were still free but on the cusp of being real grown-ups. We had no way of knowing, but only a few years later we would both be wives and mothers and something that impetuous could never be a possibility.

When Salinger died twelve years later, Vanessa gave me a first edition of his short stories, which I treasure to this day. And while we make new memories every day with our kids attending the same schools, that rural road trip remains a time capsule of a long-gone side of our personalities. Don't get me wrong—we are still kooky and adventuresome, but we just don't do interstate stalking. Thank goodness not all the nuts are in the nuthouse.

SHARK WEEK

WHO WOULD SWIM WITH SHARKS ON PURPOSE ?! MY HUSBAND.

Through my decades living on the Upper East Side and then meeting kids in boarding school from what one person called "the platinum triangle of Locust Valley, Greenwich, and Hobe Sound," I have been exposed, often via eavesdrop, to a phenomenon of this rarefied milieu: Rich People Accidents.

On *Odd Mom Out,* the character Vanessa, who is an ER doctor, has attended patients with quintessentially Upper East Side maladies: one woman was hyperventilating into a Ladurée bag after kindergarten admissions letters went out, and another had her three-thousand-dollar Indian hair extensions stuck in a Pilates reformer. Had time permitted, we might have had her experience other very true rich people accidents I've heard about: the rupture of a breast implant on the Concorde, a medevac for a guy who crashed his Ferrari, or seeing someone choke on frogs' legs.

Sadly, many Rich Person Accidents can result in Rich People *Deaths.* Such was the case for how we got the idea for my *Odd*

Mom Out father-in-law's demise—leaving Candace the merry widow, in their penthouse. Well, I will share that with you!

When I was growing up, I heard many tales of people my not particularly athletic (though good skiers!) parents had known who perished on various adventures, from a classmate of my mom's at the Lycée Français who went mountain climbing in Nepal and fell to his death, to an acquaintance of my dad's who was skydiving and met the same fate. The basic underlying tone to my parents' retelling of these tragedies was *Jews don't do that shit.*

You didn't have to tell me! I never understood what would possess someone to jump out of a plane. Perhaps, I thought to myself, they think life is so easy and they are so privileged that they are somehow dead inside and just want to feel alive. Maybe the challenge releases adrenaline and it's like a drug to them, rather than, say, a nice meal with wine. Or some pills. Either way, I have never been able to wrap my brain around it, and actually equate it with mild stupidity and hubris in the face of the fragility of life.

And then . . . I met Harry. My husband is an adrenaline junkie, and if that is an addiction, then the gateway drug was his skiing (recall the AMF slope he almost killed me on). But as with illegal substances, a person's tolerance grows as time passes and fetishes are fed. So now regular skiing—even the hardest slopes—doesn't get him off. Now he goes helicopter skiing.

When Harry first signed up, I was dead against it. My dad had regaled my brother and me with a horrible Rich Person Accident story about a group of people he knew who went helicopter skiing and were crushed by a massive avalanche that wiped out the entire posse. Lovely. But Harry would be with a group I trusted, and so many other people we kind of knew had helicopter-skied safely, so I relented.

Parasailing, skydiving, and paraskiing followed (the last one with myself included on tandem—shat m' pants), but the biggie was the final box to check on the bucket list: swimming with great white sharks.

I laughed it off for a while; I mean, really, of all the vacation options on erf did we seriously have to plan a *Jaws* voyage? As luck would have it, Harry got the opportunity to kill two birds with one stone. One day we received a save-the-date for a wedding outside Cape Town in the wine country of Constantia, South Africa. Awesome. A few minutes later, I thought Harry was on the computer, booking just flights and our hotel, but then I saw photos of his jagged-toothed friends on his screen. "Um . . . hi," I probed. "What the fuck is that?"

"Gansbaai, South Africa, has the highest concentration of great whites in the world," he said, beaming. "It's only six hours from where we are going to be!"

"I'm sorry, *only* six hours? That's, like, another country."

"I'm not going to Cape Town and missing this. It's my one chance to swim with great white sharks, and the best crew in the world is there to take me."

As it turns out, the dudes we hired had also taken Peter Benchley when he was researching *Jaws* and they took countless Nat-Geo peeps and appeared to be *the* people in shark watching. Fuck.

We hauled ass to SoAfs via London, in the last row of coach, where the seats didn't go back, right next to the shitter. It was the single most torturous flight of my life—and I say that having flown for years with kids and this was just the two of us. Exhausted and sore from being origamied into a sardine can of a seat, we arrived and checked in, showered, had an early dinner, and went to bed so we could get up before dawn for our colossal schlep to our possible deaths.

The bus ride was interminable and I was filled with dread.

Talk about Rich People Accidental Deaths. Harry was courting it! He was going to ruin my friend's wedding weekend by getting devoured. And on top of that, when I came back to New York, people wouldn't even pity my widow status. They'd say, *Well, he swam with sharks, what do you expect?* Others would probably whisper that I was a shit wife because I'd *allowed* my partner to descend to a watery grave. I became more and more stressed and reminded myself that the website was professional and the testimonials on it had been glowing. I figured I'd be able to exhale when we got there.

No such luck.

We pulled up to a house that can only be described—and I am being generous—as a shitbox. It was a ramshackle single-story unit that appeared to be prefab with three picnic tables outside. We were led across the patio and asked to take a seat next to other intrepid murderous-fish chasers. Then our leader got up to brief us about the adventure ahead. As he was talking about his pedigree, one of his colleagues began circulating packets, placing one in front of each of us on the picnic tables. A couple other people—all kind of hippie looking—came out with trays of warm bottled water, sad-looking salad, and gross bulky sandwiches that they placed on an adjacent table. Our pricey package had included a "chef-cooked meal," but judging by the hideous buffet, the chef's last name was Boyardee.

We were asked to read the contents of the contract before us, and sign the last page. The lettering was so tiny that even with my twenty-twenty vision I couldn't decipher the legalese. I did see various phrases that seemed to jump out like fish, such as "sustained injuries," "indemnity," and "in the event of death." Basically I signed my life away with a Bic ballpoint pen on a picnic table.

"And lastly, ladies in the group, I'll need you to raise your hand if you are menstruating!"

I spat out my water. Luckily I was not surfing the crimson tide. That would have sucked, to admit it to a group of total strangers, but whatevskis. Bullet dodged. It was time to eat.

I tried to force-feed myself some brown-edged lettuce leaves and a bite of sandwich, but I wasn't feeling so hot. My husband and all the other guys happily chowed down.

I looked over and could have sworn I saw the crew of our boat smoking pot. I told Harry, who blew it off, and so I asked one of the other guys.

"I'm sorry, but . . . is that marijuana?"

"No, they're hand-rolled cigarettes," he protested.

Weird, because I know what pot smells like—I despise the smell—and I knew I was smelling it. We were all going to die.

"Let me guess," the leader said, putting his hand on my arm. "New Yorker?"

His chill accent, seaside swagger, and sun-kissed skin all signified an easygoing life, another world from the one I orbited in at home. I nodded yes ashamedly, as clearly my neuroses were a pattern of 212 women. I hated being labeled that easily.

"Darlin', we've been doing this for decades. You don't have to worry!"

He reclined on the bench, propped up with his hand, and I recall thinking if he were any more laid-back he'd fall on the patio floor.

Next, we broke into groups and were taken to our vessels. After a quick safety lesson for the divers (I was not one—I would watch from the boat, thank you very much), we motored out toward Shark Alley.

We sat alongside buckets of chum, which was soon thrown

around the perimeter of the boat to attract the stars of the show. It worked instantly; within a minute I yelled, *"There's one of those triangles!"* and started to sing the *Jaws* theme. The guy looked at me and rolled his eyes. "You think you're the first one to sing that?" Ouch. Sowwy!

One dorsal fin soon became five, and they were circling us like synchronized swimmers. I begged Harry not to go.

"This is insane. Why would you go down there with them in a wire cage?"

"Sweetie, you're being paranoid. These guys are pros!"

They led him to his cage in his suit and scuba gear. He looked like an anorexic seal in a seven-foot vertical coffin made of chicken wire. They lowered him down and threw chum right next to his cage. Two sharks started ramming his cage. I got busy trying to stifle screams to avoid looking like a Manhattan nutcase. So far so good. I breathed deeply. I was *just* starting to feel calm when I heard one of the Phish-blaring bros start *screaming*.

"THE TOP OF THE CAGE HAS COME UNDONE!"

There were choruses of frightened "HOLY SHEET!" (That was the "Soth Efrica" pronunciation.)

The blood drained from my face and I went into a full-fledged panic. The other divers ran to the side to watch, probably secretly hoping for blood to bubble up. It's a miracle that I didn't diarrhea right then and there on the deck, as the whole crew *froke* and were calling to each other and in a frenzy, started cranking the cage back up to the boat. *Two fourteen-foot* sharks rammed repeatedly against Harry's cage, which had a faulty hinge that had somehow opened during said ramming.

These formerly overly chill and possibly on-pot hippies went from Grateful Dead to Almost Dead from my wrath. But I stopped screaming at them when my husband fell aboard, took off his mask, and vomited all over the place. When he was all done with bulky sandwich-remain chunders, he wiped off his mouth, looked up at me, and said, "That was awesome!"

Ridick. I was expecting a teary apology for putting me through that, but nay. And the near-fatal cage malfunction didn't stop the outing either! One of the other divers chickened out, but another went down in the other (nonbroken) cage. He came up so shaken that his vomit didn't cease until we reached land. I tried to touch his back and ask if he was okay, and he turned around and snapped at me, *"No, I'm not okay?!"* Sheesh. What a pussy. Granted, I would never do that shit, but my Harry had, and in a fucked-up cage no less. He looked like a champ next to this dude.

I am grateful Harry didn't actually kick the bucket while checking that off the bucket list. It's back to being normal people who don't put ourselves in harm's way. For now.

Listen, I know that I could probably just as easily be killed crossing Sixty-second Street and expire as diners at Mon Petit Café watch me bleed to death. But seeing Harry almost become chum himself reminded me yet again how fragile life is. I say why throw rocks at that delicate balance by risking it all so brazenly? It's not smart to be a dick tease to the Grim Reaper. Okay, maybe he doesn't have a wiener under that cloak, but he definitely wields a scythe. So enjoy what you have, be the anti-Icarus, and relish your feet on the ground before you inevitably wind up in it.

Acknowledgments

At a party I ran into the incredible Alina Cho, who told me about her new gig finding authors at Penguin Random House, two days before I was going to shop this to other publishers. I don't believe in fate, but it was fortuitous, since she led me to the amazing team at Ballantine Books. My editor, Marnie Cochran, is a superstar who put up with my made-up words, font-stickler issues, and cheesephobia about the cover. Thanks to her and the fabulous shutterbug Deborah Feingold, plus the whole pub posse: Susan Corcoran; Quinne Rogers; Kim Hovey; Cindy Murray; Jennifer Hershey; Denise Cronin; and our fearless leader, Kara Welsh.

Thank you to the best agent on earth, Jennifer Joel, sage adviser and friend, plus Ayala Cohen and the whole ICM crew, including Sean Liebowitz, Diana Glazer, Brittany Perlmuter, and Sharon Green. Thank you also to my lawyer of two decades (!), Steven Beer of Franklin, Weinrib, Rudell, and Vassallo.

To my best friends, the sisters I never had who keep me laughing: Vanessa Eastman, Dr. Lisa Turvey, Jeannie Stern, Lauren Duff, Alexis Hilton, Dana Jones, I love you so much. Trip Cullman, my partner in crime and best godfather on earth, thank you for always supporting me. A special thank you to Brittany Beeson and Vernette Lochan for all your support and patience. Thanks as well to killer book party hostesses Marcie Pantzer, Jenn Linardos, and Cindy Milazzo.

To my *Odd Mom Out* family, led by Lara Spotts, Julie Rottenberg, and Elisa Zuritsky, you made me realize how lonely it is writing a book—I missed our writers' room and camaraderie the whole time and I cherish our li'l show with all my heart.

Lastly to all of my Kopelman family, with extra kisses to Mom, Dad, Will, and Drew: You are teachers on how to live life, and make me so happy. And to all the Kargmans, especially Harry, Sadie, Ivy, and Fletch: You make life worth living, and all our adventures and laughter bring glitter to each day. I love you so.

About the Author

JILL KARGMAN is the writer and star of the hit Bravo television show *Odd Mom Out,* based on her novel *Momzillas.* She is also the *New York Times* bestselling author of *The Ex-Mrs. Hedgefund,* three novels for young readers, and the essay collection *Sometimes I Feel Like a Nut.* She has written for *Vogue, Elle, Harper's Bazaar, GQ,* and many other magazines, was a columnist for Style.com, and wrote for the MTV shows *So Five Minutes Ago* and *Who Is.* Kargman is a graduate of Yale University. Married and the mother of three, she lives in Manhattan.

jillkargman.com
@jillkargman
bravotv.com/odd-mom-out

About the Type

This book was set in a Monotype face called Bell. The Englishman John Bell (1745–1831) was responsible for the original cutting of this design. The vocations of Bell were many—bookseller, printer, publisher, typefounder, and journalist, among others. His types were considerably influenced by the delicacy and beauty of the French copperplate engravers. Monotype Bell might also be classified as a delicate and refined rendering of Scotch Roman.